VIETNAMESE
COOKING

Recipes My Mother Taught Me

ANH THU STUART

GRILLED PORK BALLS
(Nem Nuong) recipe p. 27

VIETNAMESE
COOKING

Recipes My Mother Taught Me

ANH THU STUART

To Eliane, James and Alexander

CORNSTALK PUBLISHING
An imprint of CollinsAngus&Robertson Publishers Pty Limited

First published in Australia by Angus & Robertson Publishers in 1986
First published in the United Kingdom by Angus & Robertson (UK) in 1986
Reprinted in 1987
This Cornstalk edition published in Australia in 1991 by
CollinsAngus&Robertson Publishers Pty Limited (ACN 009 913 517)
A division of HarperCollinsPublishers (Australia) Pty Limited
Unit 4, Eden Park, 31 Waterloo Road, North Ryde
NSW 2113, Australia

William Collins Publishers Ltd
31 View Road, Glenfield, Auckland 10, New Zealand

Angus & Robertson (UK)
77-85 Fulham Palace Road, London W6 8JB, United Kingdom

National Library of Australia
Cataloguing-in-Publication data:

Stuart, Anh Thu.
   Vietnamese cooking.

   Includes index.
   ISBN 0 207 15347 7

   1. Cookery, Vietnamese. I. Title

641.59597

Cover photograph Per Ericson
Typeset in Bembo by Midland Typesetters
Printed in Singapore

6   5   4   3
95 94 93 92 91

Contents

Note:
MONOSODIUM GLUTAMATE (MSG)
As it is not an essential ingredient,
its use in the recipes is marked
'optional'.
Once widely used as a flavour
enhancer, its value as a food additive
is now questioned and therefore
not recommended.

SPRING ROLLS
(Cha Gio) recipe p. 34

Preface

This book of recipes is a collaborative effort between myself and my mother, Madame Nguyen thi Thao, who now lives in Bordeaux, France. My mother acquired her expertise in Vietnamese cooking primarily in the traditional way, that is by learning in the kitchen from her mother and aunts. She also attended official cooking classes in Saigon.

I conceived the idea of a collaborative cookbook in 1980. This idea was prompted by several factors. The influx of Vietnamese refugees after 1975 led to the opening of many Vietnamese restaurants here and a growing appreciation of Vietnamese cuisine by Westerners, but there was still no sign of any specialist Vietnamese cookbooks outside Vietnam. The deciding factor was my friends' appreciation of my cooking and their suggestions that I should put my recipes into print. An additional incentive was the thought that a Vietnamese cookbook could help increase Westerners' understanding of Vietnamese people and culture.

My foremost thanks go to my parents, without whose help I could not have written this cookbook. Secondly, I owe much to Roger Stuart for his editorial contribution and his encouragement and his reprimands as I struggled to complete the project. I thank my daughter Eliane for her generous help, Celia Westwood and Sharon Coady for helping with the typing and providing editorial comments, and David Marr for his assistance with the introductory chapter. I am most grateful to Kerry Regan and Jessie Stuart for their editorial help. Finally, I thank Margaret Gleeson, not only for her comments on the manuscript, but also for being an unfailingly enthusiastic 'tester' of many of the recipes.

SOUR FISH SOUP
(Ca Nau Chua) recipe p. 47

PRAWNS FRIED IN FISH SAUCE
(Tom Riem Nuoc Mam) recipe p. 44

Introduction

This book is for the newcomer to Vietnamese cuisine as well as for the experienced cook. It will introduce Westerners to our methods of cooking and I hope it will provide a useful guide to the menus of Vietnamese restaurants. It will also help those of us who, like me, are away from our country of origin, to recapture the flavours of Vietnam.

The recipes are arranged according to their main ingredients: vegetables, pork, seafood, poultry, beef, soups and noodles. I have not included a section on desserts and cakes. Although there is a wide variety of Vietnamese cakes and sweet condiments, desserts are not a traditional feature of Vietnamese meals; in Vietnam meals are usually completed with a piece of fresh tropical fruit. Cakes and sweet dishes are usually eaten as snacks between meals or, occasionally, as appetisers. Vietnamese sweets are complicated to prepare and can sometimes take days to make. For these reasons I decided that, important and delicious though they are, Vietnamese sweet dishes and condiments are beyond the scope of this book. I hope to be able in the future to publish a second volume covering this area.

The most difficult aspects of writing this book have been controlling my nostalgia and keeping my mouth from watering at each line of each recipe. Food is a necessity of life, but at the same time it has the magical power of bringing to memory experiences associated with that dish in the past. For a Vietnamese or past visitor to Vietnam, the taste of *pho*, a popular soup, can suddenly unscroll in the mind a scene of the everyday life of Saigon: the foodstalls, the tree-lined boulevards filled with 'cyclos', little Renault taxis, motorbikes and pushbikes, the constant street-noise, the shoeshine boys, the women elegantly dressed in their *ao dai*.

The cuisine of a country contributes to its culture just as much as do art, music and costume. This is certainly true of Vietnam, whose cookery has developed over the thousands of years of its history. Unfortunately this part of Vietnam's cultural heritage has been rather ignored in the recent past; since 1945 in particular, war and politics, rather than culture, have provided the main foci of international interest in Vietnam. I hope that this cookbook will help make up for this imbalance by contributing something to an understanding of Vietnam's culture and people.

The book contains recipes from the three regions of Vietnam: North, Centre and South. The emphasis, however, is on the dishes of Southern Vietnam where I was born and then lived for the first eighteen years of my life.

AUTHOR'S BACKGROUND

I was born and spent my early childhood in the Mekong Delta. The Delta is famous as the 'rice bowl' of Vietnam, and rice is the staple of the Vietnamese diet as well as being the single most important economic and cultural commodity. Fish, pork, poultry (particularly duck), fruits and vegetables exist in good supply in the region and form the basis of a varied regional cuisine.

My parents were teachers in our village. Later they were to become headmaster and headmistress

Madame Nguyen thi Thao, the author's mother

woman in transition. But although she became a professional woman in her own right, in the eyes of my father's family she was above all a daughter-in-law. From that perspective her cooking talent was the most essential quality for earning respect. Thus my mother had the double burden of being a school headmistress during school terms and a daughter-in-law-cum-cook in the school holidays.

She resented these demands upon her, and was determined that my sister and I should not have the same experience. When it was time for us to start school she insisted that we receive a modern education to increase our chances of going to university and having professions in our own right. At that time, even though the French had relinquished their colonial prerogatives years earlier, French schools were considered by the Vietnamese middle class to provide the best kind of education and the best opportunities for university and career prospects. For this reason we were sent to a French school in Saigon. At the same time, however, we received a traditional education at home.

But despite her modernity my mother continued to hold, in a somewhat contradictory manner, some very traditional beliefs. She maintained, for example, that 'the way to a man's heart is through his stomach'. When I reached my teens I was repeatedly told to go to the kitchen to watch either my mother or the cook preparing the evening meals. Sometimes I had to prepare the dinner myself. I found these tasks, which often took me away from my latest French or Vietnamese novel, rather tedious and boring.

Little did I know then that many years later, in Australia, when my stomach had had enough of lamb chops and my mind was yearning for things past, I would thankfully call upon those skills so unwillingly acquired.

of primary schools in Saigon. They both came from rural backgrounds, with my grandparents on both sides being small farmers. My paternal grandfather was also the village herbal doctor. Thus my family background was very traditional. One aspect of this conservatism was that women were expected to conform to the Confucian dogmas. In work the woman had to master cooking, sewing and embroidery, but normally not reading or writing. In physical appearance she had to be attractive to her husband, but not enticing to others. In speech she had to be modest and exceedingly polite, rather than assertive or imaginative. And in behaviour she had always to be respectful of, and dutiful to her 'superiors'.

My mother managed largely to escape this prison of tradition; she was the modern Vietnamese

MEALS OF THE DAY

Many friends of Vietnam often make jokes about the eating habits of its people; they often wonder whether Vietnamese ever stop eating. In our family we had three main meals a day, not counting the occasional visits to the local foodstalls in between meals.

Our day would begin with a hearty breakfast. We could choose from a wide range of dishes from the local foodstalls: *pho*, a rice noodle soup; or *banh cuon cha lua*, rice pancake and meat loaf served with mung bean sprouts and special fish sauce; or *xoi*, glutinous rice with mung beans or red beans; or French bread with roast pork. Our relatives in the countryside, on the other hand, had less choice. Their breakfast was invariably based on rice: boiled rice eaten with leftovers from yesterday's meals, or *xoi*, glutinous rice.

At lunchtime, like all school children, we had to go home to join other members of our family for the main meal of the day. It consisted of three dishes: soup, vegetables and a meat or fish dish served together at the table with boiled rice. There was no distinction between courses. This was followed by an hour-long siesta.

Our family, like most Vietnamese families, had its biggest meal in the middle of the day. However, our evening meal was not that much different from the midday meal. It, too, was based on boiled rice accompanied by soup, a vegetable dish and a fish or meat dish. Meat was rather expensive and therefore served sparingly.

The common weekday meals described above were generally quick and easy to prepare. The Sunday meals, on the other hand, were more complex. In our family, Sunday lunch was always the most special and delicious meal of the week. Just as Westerners traditionally have made Sunday lunch special by cooking a roast, my mother used to create a sense of occasion at this meal by preparing more complicated and expensive dishes such as *banh xeo* (seafood pancake), *nem nuong* (grilled pork balls) and *chao tom* (grilled prawn balls).

FESTIVITIES AND BANQUETS

In the Vietnam of my childhood the most memorable events of life, birth, marriage and death, were associated with food. At each of these occasions food was offered to the ancestors at the family altar. Great thought and care were given to the preparation and presentation of these offerings, and for each type of occasion there was a particular dish. Occasions such as anniversaries of the dead also provided a venue for meeting and reminiscing with relatives and friends; they were not mournful events. The meal and conversation were essential parts of the ceremony. So were the children playing in the yard, for traditionally children were not excluded from formal occasions such as banquets, weddings or anniversaries of the dead. Maybe it is our early introduction to such fine meals on these occasions that has made us so appreciative of our food.

On such occasions various dishes were served separately as distinctive courses, thereby increasing the formality of the events. The banquets would sometimes extend to more than ten courses.

Our approach to the preparation of food was also strongly aesthetic. Food had to be presented in the most attractive way possible; the more colourful and natural the better. One particular dish comes to mind, the *goi sua* or jellyfish salad, which has at least five colours: the yellow of the jellyfish, the grey of the cooked pork, the pink of the cooked prawn, the white of the cucumber slices, the red of the chillies and the green of the spring onions. The chillies and spring onions are also transformed by the cook into delicately carved red and green 'flowers'. A cook in Vietnam should also be an artist.

REGIONAL DIFFERENCES

Connoisseurs of Vietnamese cuisine will be familiar with its distinctive qualities. These include:

- **the extensive use of fresh vegetables and herbs such as coriander and mint**
- **the restrained use of frying and thickening**
- **the use of a variety of sauces based on soya beans and fish extract**
- **the use of *banh trang*, a wafer made from rice flour and sometimes covered with sesame seed.**

But the most distinctive characteristic of Vietnamese cooking is the extensive use of fish sauce — *nuoc mam*. This is used for seasoning in a way similar to that of soya sauce in Japan and China. But because it is not as dark as soya sauce, *nuoc mam* allows food to retain a fresher colour.

However, there are marked differences in the cooking styles of the three regions of Vietnam. The variations are due very largely to the different types of ingredients which are available, and these are influenced in turn by climatic and soil differences. The different historical backgrounds of the regions have also contributed. For example, the presence of the Cham people in Central Vietnam and the Khmer in Southern Vietnam have imparted distinctive Thai and Kampuchean qualities to the cuisine of those two regions. This helps account, for example, for the extensive use of fish sauce and fermented fish in the South.

Northern Vietnam is well known for its *pho* and *bun thang*, two noodle soup dishes. Vietnamese from the North also eat a lot of *rau muong*, a spinach-like vegetable that grows on water.

The range of dishes available in Southern Vietnam is much wider than in any other region. Its dishes are predominantly based on fish and other seafood. Chillies are used generously. Visitors to Southern Vietnam will remember its *banh xeo* (Vietnamese pancake), *chao tom* (prawn balls) and *tom cang nuong* (grilled lobster).

Central Vietnam, being the poorest region of the three, does not offer as much variety. It distinguishes itself with various types of fish stewed in fish sauce, called *ca kho. Bun bo Hue* (noodle soup from Hue) comes, as its name indicates, from the traditional royal capital of Vietnam.

Because of the extensive migration between regions over the centuries it is difficult to determine confidently the origins of many of the dishes. I am sure that Vietnamese from each region would claim many dishes as their own. For this reason I have not categorised recipes by region.

FOREIGN INFLUENCES

Another distinguishing feature of Vietnamese cuisine is the way in which it has absorbed certain features of other cooking traditions. Vietnamese cuisine has been influenced in particular by Chinese, Indian, Malay and French cooking.

The Chinese influence has been the strongest. Many dishes were introduced to Vietnam by the Chinese and still retain a Chinese quality. Nevertheless, over the centuries they have acquired a distinctively Vietnamese flavour and have become an integral part of our diet.

The French introduced to Vietnamese cuisine the use of butter, bread and many temperate climate vegetables such as cauliflowers, carrots, peas and potatoes. To this day Vietnamese still give pidgin names to these vegetables.

The presence of curry dishes in Vietnamese cooking must have resulted from the migration of Indians into Vietnam. They were brought to Vietnam by the French following the colonisation of the country. However, the curry dishes also have a distinctively Malay flavour because of the extensive use of coconut milk. The curry paste is locally made by Indians. To this day I have not tasted curries that would equal in flavour and aroma those that my mother used to make.

PANCAKES WITH BEAN SPROUTS, PORK AND PRAWNS
(Banh Xeo) recipe p.80

COCONUT MILK
(Nuoc Dua)

BEAN SAUCE
(Nuoc Tuong Hot)

FISH SAUCE
(Nuoc Mam)

RICE PAPER
(Banh Trang)

CHILLIES
(Ot)

CHINESE MUSHROOMS
(Nam Dong Co)

SHELLED MUNG BEANS
(Dau Xanh)

RICE FLOUR
(Bot Gao)

VIETNAMESE MINT
(Rau Ram)

CHINESE NOODLES
(Mi)

RICE VERMICELLI
(Bun)

RICE NOODLES
(Banh Pho)

Glossary of Ingredients

A

aniseed *(tay vi)*
the seed of the anise, a brown, dried, star-shaped clove with a fragrance like dill (star anise)
anisette *(ruou anis)*
a liqueur flavoured with aniseed

B

bamboo shoots *(mang tre)*
crunchy, creamy-coloured shoots of bamboo which are cut when they grow to about 20 cm above ground. In Vietnam they are always available fresh. In our house our supply of bamboo shoots came from our own plants in the backyard. The green outer part must be removed and the inside boiled in water with a dash of salt before being used. Outside Asia they are mainly available in tins. They should be well washed before use.
bac ha
a typically Vietnamese vegetable with green stalks, used for stir frying or in soup. Available from Chinese food stores. Can be replaced with celery.
basil *(rau que)*
a herb with a spicy and aromatic fragrance, eaten fresh or with soup. This herb can be grown easily at home. Keep the herb in a pot inside in winter.
bean curd *(dau hu)*
a mild-flavoured product made from mashed and cooked soya beans pressed into cakes. Three types of bean curd are available:
- a plain white custard-like product *(dau hu chung)*
- a brown looking fried bean curd with a mild nutty flavour *(dau hu chien)*
- dried bean curd *(dau hu ki)*

It is a good source of protein and needs very little cooking because it is already cooked. Do not let its blandness discourage you from using it. It absorbs the stronger flavours of other ingredients and as a result can possess a range of distinctive and attractive flavours.
bean sprouts *(gia)*
sprouts from mung beans which are soaked in water to germinate. They are crunchy and can be eaten stir-fried or raw in salads. Many Vietnamese families living outside Vietnam grow their own bean sprouts indoors. However, bean sprouts are usually available from Chinese food stores. They are also sold at some greengrocers and large supermarkets. When buying these sprouts make sure that they are not limp and stale.
bean sauce *(nuoc tuong hot)*
a salty brown bean paste made from soya beans which forms the basis for dip sauces in Vietnamese cooking. It is sold tinned or in jars, with whole or ground beans. The refined or ground bean sauce is used for making sauce for dipping.

C

caramel sauce *(nuoc mau)*
a liquid preparation made from caramelised sugar (see p. 89 for method). It is primarily used for aesthetic reasons, to give a golden brown appearance to meat and chicken. Whenever I run out of this sauce I replace it with a teaspoon of dark thick soya sauce (see p. 10) or treacle.
caraway mint *(rau la tia to)*
a pungent and spicy herb grown from caraway seeds. The leaves are round shaped and of a green and purple colour. It is eaten raw with salad. It may be hard to obtain from shops but can be replaced by ordinary mint.
celery leaves *(rau can)*
the leaves as well as the stalks of celery are used in Vietnamese cooking. They have a special aromatic flavour that blends in well with stir-fried vegetables or soup.
char siu powder *(bot xa xiu)*
a powder mixture mainly composed of five spice

powder (q.v.) and red colouring. It is used for roasting pork.

chillies *(ot)*
a hot variety of the capsicum family. Chillies can be obtained fresh from Chinese stores, greengrocers and supermarkets. The smaller chillies are hotter than large ones. In Vietnam they are called *ot hiem* i.e. 'mean chillies'! If fresh chillies are not available they can be replaced by dried chillies.

Chinese cabbage *(rau cai tau)*
this vegetable has large, curly dark green leaves and long stems which are firmly closed together to form a firm thick bunch. It is available in Chinese grocery stores. The leaves taste slightly bitter, rather like spinach.

Chinese mushrooms *(nam dong co)*
available dried from Chinese grocery stores. They are dark brown in colour and require soaking in hot water before use.

Chinese dried plums *(tao do)*
similar in look to the western plum but quite different in flavour and texture. It is mainly used for slow cooking in soups or stuffings for chicken.

Chinese noodles
(see noodles)

coconut, freshly grated *(dua nao)*
made from fresh coconut flesh either by manual grating or by using a food processor

coconut, desiccated *(dua nao kho)*
dried grated coconut flesh, readily available in supermarkets

coconut juice *(nuoc dua tuoi)*
juice from the coconut. In Vietnam it is a most refreshing drink when the coconut is still green and fresh off the tree. Coconut juice is also widely used with rice or chicken to give them a special aromatic sweet flavour.

coconut milk *(nuoc cot dua)*
made from coconut flesh (see p. 14 for recipe)

coriander leaves *(rau ngo)*
a green herb with a very strong and aromatic flavour, not to be confused with parsley. It is used with chopped spring onions as garnish for most stir-fried and soup dishes. It can be obtained from Chinese grocery shops. However it can also be grown in spring and summer from coriander seeds. Make sure the plants get the morning sun and plenty of water.

curry leaves *(la ca-ri)*
small leaves used to flavour curry dishes. Available in dried form only. Bay leaves can be used as a substitute.

F

fish sauce *(nuoc mam)*
a liquid preparation extracted from fish marinated in salt. Layers of raw fish alternating with layers of salt are left to ferment in wooden boxes for up to six months. The fish liquid extract is then filtered down, boiled and mixed with some special natural colouring. Fish sauce is produced in various coastal regions of Vietnam from North to South. It varies from region to region depending on the type of fish and technique used. The best fish sauce reputedly comes from the island of Phu-Quoc and is based on a freshwater fish called *ca com*. The process of making fish sauce is a Vietnamese traditional art which is handed from generation to generation.

five spice powder *(ngu vi huong)*
a dark brown ready-mixed powder containing aniseed, anise pepper, fennel, cloves and cinnamon. It is used to season meat and poultry. It has a very strong aroma and should be used only sparingly.

G

garlic *(toi)*
this bulb belonging to the onion family is well known to most Western cooks. It is used in most Vietnamese recipes and emits a most attractive aroma when fried or grilled with meat. As mentioned previously, to prepare garlic, use flat side of a cleaver to flatten and break the cloves. Remove skin and chop roughly with sharp end. This method enables the garlic to retain its aroma better than the use of the garlic squeezer.

ginger *(gung)*
the root of the ginger plant. It is always used fresh in Vietnamese cooking and should be tender and juicy. It must be peeled before use. It is available at most greengrocers.

ginkgo nut *(bac cua)*
a Chinese nut used in soups and stuffing for poultry. Needs to be shelled and blanched. Also available canned.

golden needles *(kim cham)*
(see lily buds)

H
he
a typically Asian vegetable with long, flat, thin green stems. It has a strong flavour and can be eaten raw or cooked. It is sometimes available at Chinese grocery stores.
hoisin sauce *(tuong ngot)*
a thick spicy soya bean based sauce. Used as a dip sauce.

J
jellyfish *(sua)*
salted jellyfish strips are available from Chinese grocery stores. They should be boiled and cooled down before use in salads. They have a particularly crunchy texture.

L
lemon grass *(xa)*
a grasslike plant with a bulbous base end with the fragrance of lemon. It is an important herb in Vietnamese cooking. The bottom part of the stalk (about 15 cm) is used to flavour dishes. Use whole for braising or finely chopped for frying. It can be obtained fresh from Chinese food stores. Dried lemon grass can also be used instead.
lily buds *(kim cham)*
a golden yellow dried flower. Remove the stamens and then soak petals before using with meats or vegetables.

M
mint, caraway
(see caraway mint)
mint, Vietnamese
(see Vietnamese mint)
monosodium glutamate (MSG) *(bot ngot)*
a powder used to improve the flavour of certain dishes, mainly soup. As it is not an essential ingredient, its use in the recipe is marked 'optional'. Once widely used as a flavour enhancer, its value as a food additive is now questioned and therefore not recommended. Can be replaced by a chicken stock cube.
mung beans *(dau xanh)*
dried peas similar to lentils with green shells and

yellow cores, used in sauces and sweets. Also used for growing bean sprouts.
mung bean vermicelli *(bun tau)*
transparent noodles made from mung bean flour. Need to be soaked in warm water before cooking. Available at Chinese food stores.
mint *(rau hun cay)*
European mint, an aromatic herb used mainly in salads and sometimes as a garnish.

N
noodles *(mi)*
refers to Chinese wheat-flour noodles that can be obtained fresh or dried at the Chinese grocery store
noodles, rice
(see rice noodles)

O
onion *(hanh)*
use brown onions in preference to white onions. To prepare for stir-fry method cut in half lengthwise and then cut into segments as with oranges.
oyster sauce *(dau hao)*
a thick grey-brown sauce made from oysters and soya sauce, used for flavouring meats and poultry.

P
potassium nitrate
chemical used to preserve meat and to give it a pink colour when cooked.
potato flour
flour made from potatoes. It is readily available.
prawn crackers *(banh phong tom)*
crisp slices made from the batter of dried prawns. Available in packets from Chinese grocery stores. Fry in hot oil, one at a time, for 5-10 seconds, until puffed up. Do not overcook.

R
rice *(gao* when uncooked, *com* when cooked)
use long grain variety. See p. 13 for cooking method.
rice flour *(bot gao)*
made from ordinary rice
rice flour, glutinous *(bot nep)*
made from glutinous rice.
rice, glutinous *(nep* when uncooked, *xoi* when cooked)
a rounder grain rice which becomes sticky when

cooked. It is very rich and is eaten sparingly. It is often cooked with shelled mung beans.

rice, ground roasted *(thin)*
obtained by first dry frying the rice in a thick-based frying pan. After the rice turns light brown it is ground in a coffee grinder or with a mortar and pestle. The result is a light brown coarse powder with a distinctive aroma. It is used with some pork dishes.

rice noodles *(hu tieu* or *banh pho)*
noodles made from rice flour. They are available dried in packages at Chinese grocery stores.

rice paper *(banh trang)*
made from rice flour and then dried until crisp. Available in many sizes from Chinese food stores. Before using dampen with warm water one at a time and spread on a clean tea-towel.

rice vermicelli *(bun)*
vermicelli made from rice flour. They are available dried in three sizes: thin, medium and thick. Unless otherwise stated the term rice vermicelli in this book refers to medium-sized vermicelli.

S

sesame seeds *(me)*
tiny flat seeds, usually roasted

sesame oil *(dau me)*
nutty flavoured oil, used sparingly for stir-frying

shrimp paste *(mam ruoc)*
made from prawns and salt. It has a very strong fishy smell and tastes like an anchovy paste. It should be used sparingly because it has a rather overpowering flavour.

soya sauce *(nuoc tuong)*
made from soya beans and salt, this sauce was introduced to Vietnam by the Chinese. Two varieties of soya sauce are used in Vietnamese cooking: a thin and a thick sauce. The thin sauce is light brown and used for making sauces for dipping. The thick sauce is darker — almost black — and used for cooking and colouring.

spring onions *(hanh la)*
small plant (about 40 cm long) with a white bulbous base and tubular green leaves. The base is used for cooking and the leaves are used for garnishing.

T

tamarind *(me)*
a dark brown fruit with sweet and sour flavour. Tamarind juice is obtained by soaking a heaped tablespoon of tamarinds in half a cup of warm water for 10 minutes and squeezing through a strainer. It can be replaced with lemon or vinegar mixed with sugar.

turmeric *(nghe)*
a yellow root which is usually available in a dry powder form only. In Vietnamese cooking it is mainly used for colouring.

V

vermicelli, rice
(see rice vermicelli)

vermicelli, mung bean
(see mung bean vermicelli)

Vietnamese mint *(rau ram)*
so called because of its introduction to Australia by Vietnamese migrants. It is an aromatic herb with long dark green leaves and a distinctively biting taste. It can be easily grown in any part of Australia. It can die back in winter frosts but will sprout again in the spring. It is used in salads, especially cabbage salad, and soups. I believe it is also used in other South-East Asian cooking. It can be obtained from Chinese greengrocers and can be grown by striking stalks in water and then planting.

W

water chestnut *(cu nang)*
a small round crispy sweet vegetable which when peeled looks like a small potato. It is available in tins at Chinese grocery stores.

watercress *(xa-lach xon)*
a vegetable with small dark green leaves, rich in iron. As its Vietnamese name indicates it must have been introduced by the French (*cresson* in French) to Vietnam. It is used for salads or soups.

Utensils & Methods

Many newcomers to Vietnamese cuisine imagine that special equipment and ingredients that are difficult to obtain outside Vietnam are required in Vietnamese cookery. This is a myth. Vietnamese cooking can be just as efficiently carried out in an ordinarily equipped Western kitchen as in a traditional Vietnamese kitchen. This chapter, which is an introduction to the basic methods and tools of Vietnamese cooking, will demonstrate this.

UTENSILS

When my mother was still living in Vietnam, she used to believe that Vietnamese traditional utensils were essential to good Vietnamese cooking. Since moving to France, however, she has come to the conclusion that modern electrical equipment provides wonderful labour-saving devices that are just as effective as the traditional, somewhat primitive utensils.

In this section I will describe the traditional utensils and show how most of them can be replaced by modern implements.

Chinese cleaver
and sharp kitchen knives

Vietnamese cooking is based on slicing and cutting meat and vegetables not just for the purpose of uniform cooking but also for appearance. Sharp kitchen knives and the cutting board are therefore essential basic tools.

For slicing and cutting vegetables I use a sharp, light, medium-sized kitchen knife. For slicing meat I use a very sharp carving knife.

For chopping meat, and especially chicken, I use a Chinese cleaver. This is a large, heavy, rectangular-shaped knife. There are cleavers of all sizes and weights. Some cooks use them for everything: slicing, chopping and even boning

chicken. My use of the cleaver is more restricted. I use it primarily for chopping and, occasionally, for mincing small quantities of meat or seafood. I also use the flat side of the cleaver to bruise garlic cloves to make them easy to peel and to flatten prawns before mincing them.

Mortar and pestle
or food processor and blender

In Vietnam, spices, nuts, meat and seafood are ground or crushed in a wooden or stone mortar with a pestle made of the same material. Each household would have at least two sets, the smaller set for nuts and spices and the larger one for meat and seafood.

The modern adaptations for the mortar and pestle are the electric blender and the food processor. The blender is used for spices and purees and the food processor for meat, seafood and nuts. However, because Vietnamese recipes rarely require the grinding of spices, I find that the food processor is quite adequate for my purpose.

When mincing meat or seafood care should be taken to ensure that the friction caused by the blade does not heat them up. This is the reason why in some recipes I have specified the need to cool the meat or seafood in the freezer for half an hour before using the food processor.

Nevertheless, a small mortar and pestle is a convenient implement to have in the kitchen for grinding small quantities of nuts, garlic, etc.

Wok or frying pan

All connoisseurs of Chinese cuisine will be familiar with the wok. In Vietnamese it is called *chao*. It is a large shallow bowl-shaped frying pan with a curved base. It can be made of various metals, including aluminium, iron and stainless steel, and comes in all sizes. It is a most versatile utensil. It is basically used for stir-frying. But for as long as I can remember in our family, it has been used for practically any purpose: dry frying, deep frying, steaming, frying pancakes, etc.

Because the wok is designed to be used on a traditional charcoal burner, it is not as effective on an electric stove. In a modern kitchen it is best used on a gas stove so that a large part of the wok's surface can be exposed to heat. As I live in an area where natural gas is not available, I have tended to replace the wok with an ordinary frying pan or a large casserole dish.

Charcoal burner or portable gas stove for cooking at the table

Vietnamese cook with individual earthenware charcoal burners that can also be used for cooking at the table. These burners have the shape of a small bucket and are divided into two parts: the top part for live fire and the bottom part for ashes. For cooking at the table I suggest that these be replaced by a Portagas burner which is simpler to use.

Chopsticks

To me, chopsticks are the most useful implements for stir-frying. They are also very versatile. They can be used as the equivalent of a fork for testing if the meat is cooked, tongs for picking up things, an egg-slice for turning things over and a spoon for stirring.

METHODS

Seafood cleaning techniques

The following instructions are for those who are unfamiliar with handling squid and prawns.

To clean squid

1. Holding body of squid in one hand, pull its head and tentacles gently away from its body. The intestines will automatically come away with the head.

2. Remove backbone starting from the open end of squid. It is white and light in weight.

3. If the inside of squid is still not thoroughly clean, turn hood inside out and wash under water.

4. Peel off brown outer skin.

5. Rub salt into squid and wash under cold running water thoroughly.

To clean raw prawns

1. Remove head and peel prawn starting from the underbelly.

2. Remove vein by making an incision along the back and pulling out the black thread.

3. Rub salt into prawns, mix well.

4. Wash and rinse until water is clear.

5. Drain well

Cutting and slicing techniques

Vegetables

Like most South-East Asians, Vietnamese eat a lot of vegetables. They take great care, not only in the cooking of vegetables to ensure that they retain a crunchy texture and fresh flavour, but also in their presentation at the dinner table.

Vegetables are generally sliced diagonally for salad making and cooking. Each piece should be small enough to be picked up with chopsticks and eaten whole. There are no strict rules for cutting vegetables, but it is important to cut them in a uniform way so that they can be cooked uniformly and thus retain their crunchiness throughout.

As I mentioned in the Introduction, the presentation of meals at special occasions is very important. Following are some instructions for making decorative shapes out of vegetables.

Carrot and cucumber cut into flower shapes
After peeling the vegetable cut notches in it lengthwise about 2 mm deep, and 5 mm apart. Then cut across the vegetable, and each piece looks like a flattened flower.

Chillies
Use a long sharp needle to bisect chilli (preferably red) lengthwise. Stop at about 5 mm away from stem. Remove seeds and core. Repeat process to make 8 petals. Then soak chilli in cold water. After half an hour petals will curl up, turning chilli into a flower.

Spring onion
Follow same procedure as above except for the fact that there is no core to remove.

Meat
The meat that we obtain from the butcher usually comes in large pieces. An efficient way of slicing meat is first of all to subdivide the large piece into 8 cm x 8 cm strips and then to cut across the grain of the strips one by one into slices with the required thickness.

Chicken
Most of the recipes involving chicken require chopping the chicken into bite-sized pieces before or after cooking. Following are some guides on how to cut the pieces cleanly.

Use a sharp heavy cleaver and a large and fairly thick chopping board. First remove the legs, thighs and wings from the trunk at their respective connecting joints. Then cut each leg and thigh in half. Cut the wing in half at its connecting joint and then half again if needed.

Cut the trunk in half along the middle of the sternum and the backbone. Cut each half again into two lengthwise. Place each large piece thus obtained, bones facing up, on the board and chop diagonally into 4 cm by 8 cm pieces.

How to cook rice
Rice is the staple food in Vietnam and forms the basis of most meals. It comes in many varieties with differences in flavour, texture and fragrance. White polished long grain rice is the norm. It is served plain and unsalted with other dishes.

The basic method for cooking rice consists of first boiling the rice and then simmering it. It is called the absorption or evaporation method.

Place rice in a heavy-bottomed saucepan large enough to enable the rice to expand to twice its size. Wash rice thoroughly and then change water. Repeat process two to three times until water is fairly clear. Add cold water until it is about 1.5 cm above the rice, regardless of size of saucepan.

Put lid on saucepan and bring to the boil over high heat. Remove lid, let boil for 1 to 2 minutes and reduce heat to medium. Gently stir rice with chopsticks or wooden spoon to stop rice at the bottom from sticking and burning.

With the lid loosely on, let boil for another 5 minutes or until water has all been absorbed. Reduce heat to low, cover saucepan tightly. Let the rice then cook in its own steam for another 15 to 20 minutes. Do not lift lid during this final stage, as it may lead to the rice being underdone.

The amount of water can be slightly increased if softer rice is preferred.

For some special dishes rice can also be steamed. The method of steaming the rice is described with the recipe for those particular dishes.

How to make coconut milk

First of all, we need to distinguish between coconut juice and coconut milk. Coconut juice is the clear liquid that comes from inside the coconut. Coconut milk, on the other hand, is made from grated coconut flesh.

Coconut milk is usually made from soaking grated fresh coconut flesh in warm water and then squeezing out the extract. This is a very time-consuming method as it involves removing the coconut flesh from the shell and then grating it finely. Furthermore, fresh coconuts are not always readily available. I have therefore used simpler methods of extracting coconut milk that do not involve fresh coconuts directly.

Vietnamese cooking distinguishes between thick coconut milk (*nuoc cot*, first extract) and thin coconut milk (*nuoc dao*, diluted extract). Thus coconut milk is extracted in two sequences.

1. Desiccated coconut

250 g desiccated coconut
boiling water

Put coconut in a bowl. Cover with two cups hot water and let soak for 20 minutes. Knead well, then pour coconut mixture through a fine strainer or a piece of cheesecloth. Squeeze hard to extract all the liquid.

This first extract (*nuoc cot* in Vietnamese) is the thick coconut milk that is usually kept aside to be mixed with the dish just before serving so as not to curdle the food.

After obtaining the first extract, return the desiccated coconut to the bowl. Add 2 cups hot water, let soak for 20 minutes, until cool enough to touch. Knead well then pour through fine strainer or cheesecloth. Squeeze hard to get all the milk. Repeat this process until the extracted liquid is no longer milky (about twice). This thinner extract is called *nuoc dao* in Vietnamese. Unless otherwise stated the type of coconut milk used in this book's recipes is obtained from mixing the above two types of extracts together.

2. Tinned coconut milk

This is thick coconut milk and therefore needs to be diluted with water to produce a liquid of the same consistency as the above.

3. Creamed coconut

This is a copha-like compact preparation. It comes in a small cardboard box about the size of a 250 g butter packet.

To every 30 g of coconut cream add 200 mL of hot water to make thin coconut milk. To make thick coconut milk, add only 80 mL to every 30 g.

When cooking with coconut milk it is important to follow the instructions closely so as not to curdle or burn the food.

Menu Suggestions

How to serve the meals

As I mentioned in the Introduction, an everyday meal in our family used to consist of three dishes. These were not served as separate courses but were placed together at the table to be eaten with boiled rice. The dishes were almost invariably based on vegetables, meat and fish and therefore had to be eaten together to complement each other.

On special occasions, however, the dishes would be served in sequence. Since I have been in Australia I have maintained this difference in serving methods between the everyday meal and the dinner party.

Menu suggestions

Because Vietnamese meals usually offer more than one dish at a time, I have not indicated the number of servings for each individual recipe. However, in this section I provide a number of menu suggestions together with the number of servings for the various combinations of dishes.

The menu suggestions are grouped according to the type of meal offered, the ordinary family meal or the special dinner party.

In the menus for the everyday meal, I have included dishes that are quick and easy to cook, especially on a working day. These dishes are to be eaten together and with some boiled rice.

For the dinner party menus, on the other hand, I have listed dishes that require a bit more time and skill to prepare. Unless otherwise indicated, these dishes should be eaten one at a time in the sequence shown on the menu.

Two-dish ordinary meal for four

Grilled pork chops with garlic and onion
Fried zucchini (courgettes) with crab

Fried fish in butter
Fried English spinach

Pork fried in fish sauce
Fish and tomato soup

Fried beefsteak with peanuts
Fried beans with pork and prawns

Prawns fried in fish sauce
Sweet and sour beef

Deep-fried chicken wings
Combination rice noodles fried with pork and prawns

Chicken fried in turmeric sauce
Fried mixed vegetables with pork and prawns

Fried fish in lemon grass
Fried bean sprouts with pork and prawns

Stewed leg of pork in fish sauce
Sour fish soup

Chicken in lemon grass and chilli
Stuffed cucumber

Prawns and pork fried with lemon grass
Grilled eggplant (aubergine)

Fried beef with watercress salad
Fried beans with pork and prawns

Dinner party for six

Shredded fried pork
Special steamed rice with fried chicken and vegetables

Prawns and pork rolled in rice paper
Combination fried noodles

Grilled fish with pork and rice paper
Stuffed squid (*to be eaten with boiled rice*)
Fried bean sprouts with pork and prawns (*to be eaten with boiled rice*)

Skewered beef
Sweet and sour squid (*to be eaten with boiled rice*)
Chicken in lemon grass and chilli (*to be eaten with boiled rice*)

Spring rolls
Meat and seafood fondue

Fish and tomato soup with vermicelli
Grilled pork chops with onion and garlic (*to be eaten with boiled rice*)
Fried beans with pork and prawns (*to be eaten with boiled rice*)

Deep-fried prawn toast
Chicken roasted in butter (*to be eaten with boiled rice*)
Fried mixed vegetables with pork and prawns (*to be eaten with rice*)

Grilled pork balls
Pancakes with bean sprouts, pork and prawns

Jellyfish, prawn and pork salad with prawn crackers
Fried whole chicken, Fried rice with tomato paste, and pickled bean sprouts

Deep-fried prawns in batter (*with lettuce and lemon and garlic fish sauce*)
Chicken cooked in coconut and curry sauce with vermicelli
Special fried rice

Beef stewed in lemon grass and aniseed
Chicken curry Indian style

Crab, asparagus and shark's fin soup
Prawn balls
Chicken and mushroom paella

Vegetables

Vegetables

FRIED BEAN SPROUTS WITH PORK AND PRAWNS

GIA XAO

500 g	bean sprouts
100 g	raw prawns
100 g	lean pork
	1 onion
	1 clove garlic
2 Tbsps	oil
2 Tbsps	fish sauce
½ Tsp	pepper
1 Tbsp	chopped spring onion
	1 handful coriander leaves

Wash bean sprouts and let dry in a colander.

Shell and devein prawns. Rub in 1 teaspoon salt. Wash until foam is no longer apparent in the water. Dry with paper towel.

Wash and dry pork. Slice thinly (about 2 mm thick).

Cut onion into 1 cm wide wedges. Crush garlic with the side of a chopper or large knife.

Heat oil in a large frying pan. Add onion and garlic. Stir-fry until onion turns translucent. Add pork and prawns. Stir-fry for 5 minutes until cooked. Add fish sauce and bean sprouts. Stir-fry for 2 minutes or so until bean sprouts are slightly wilted.

Sprinkle spring onion, coriander leaves and pepper on top before serving.

FRIED BEANS WITH PORK AND PRAWNS

DAU VE XAO

Follow the ingredients and procedure as for Fried Bean Sprouts With Pork and Prawns, above, but replace bean sprouts with 400 g beans.

As it takes longer to cook beans than bean sprouts, stir-fry the beans for about 5 minutes or until they change colour. Also add ½ cup water while frying beans, to stop them from burning.

FRIED ZUCCHINI (COURGETTES) WITH PORK AND PRAWNS

BAU XAO

500 g	zucchini (courgettes) *or* marrow
100 g	raw prawns
100 g	lean pork
	1 egg
	1 onion, cut into 1 cm wedges
	1 clove garlic, crushed
2 Tbsps	oil
1 Tbsp	fish sauce
1 Tsp	pepper
1 Tbsp	chopped spring onion
	1 handful coriander leaves

If using marrow or large zucchini, peel vegetables. Cut in half lengthwise. Remove some of the pith and seeds. Slice diagonally into thin pieces (about 5 mm thick) and then cut pieces into matchstick strips.

If using young zucchini, peel leaving alternate strips of green. Cut into matchstick strips.

Prepare prawns and pork as in recipe for Fried Bean Sprouts With Pork and Prawns, left.

Beat egg with a dash of fish sauce.

Heat oil in large frying pan. Add onion and garlic. Stir-fry until onion turns translucent. Add pork and prawns and half of fish sauce. Stir-fry for 5 minutes or until cooked. Add marrow and remaining fish sauce. Stir-fry for 2 minutes or until marrow turns translucent. Add egg and mix well until egg is cooked. Sprinkle pepper, spring onion and coriander leaves on top before serving. Serve hot.

Vegetables

FRIED ZUCCHINI (COURGETTES) WITH CRAB

MUOP XAO

	2 handfuls mung bean vermicelli
	1 onion
	5 zucchini (courgettes) *(about 3 cm in diameter and 25 cm long)*
2 Tbsps	oil
	1 clove garlic
100 g	crab meat
1½ Tbsps	fish sauce
1 Tsp	pepper
1 Tbsp	chopped spring onion
	1 handful coriander leaves

Soak vermicelli in warm water for 10 minutes. Remove from water, cut in half and let drain.

Cut onion into 1 cm wedges. Crush garlic.

Peel zucchini, leaving alternate strips of green. Cut into half lengthwise and then cut into slices, 5 mm thick.

Heat oil in frying pan. Add onion and garlic with a pinch of salt. Stir-fry until onion turns translucent. Add crab meat, stir-fry for 1 minute and add fish sauce and pepper. Add zucchini and stir-fry for 5 minutes until they change colour. Add about ¼ cup water to stop zucchinis from burning. Add vermicelli. Stir-fry for 2 minutes. Remove from heat.

Sprinkle spring onion, coriander leaves and pepper on top before serving. Serve hot.

GRILLED EGGPLANT (AUBERGINE)

CA TIM NUONG

	2 medium-sized eggplants (aubergines) *(choose the long thin ones)*
100 g	minced pork
	1 onion, minced
	1 clove garlic
½ Tsp	salt
1 Tsp	pepper
1 Tbsp	oil
1 Tbsp	chopped spring onion
½ cup	lemon and garlic fish sauce *(see p. 89)*

Mix pork with onion, garlic, salt and ½ teaspoon pepper.

Wash and dry eggplant. Prick with skewers right through at a few places. If eggplant is more than 6 cm thick cut in half lengthwise. Grill eggplant at medium heat. Turn over frequently to avoid burning before the vegetable is cooked.

Meanwhile heat oil in frying pan. Add pork mixture. Stir-fry until cooked.

When eggplant is tender and skin is lightly burnt, remove from heat. Place on warm plate and spread cooked pork on top. Sprinkle with spring onion and pepper. Pour lemon and garlic fish sauce on top before serving.

Vegetables

FRIED MIXED VEGETABLES WITH PORK AND PRAWNS

RAU XAO

	1 medium-sized carrot
	1 zucchini (courgette)
	¼ small cabbage
	3 celery sticks
100 g	raw prawns
100 g	lean pork
	1 onion, cut into 2 cm wedges
	1 clove garlic
2 Tbsps	oil
1 Tbsp	fish sauce
1 Tbsp	chopped spring onion
	1 handful coriander leaves
½ Tsp	pepper

Peel carrot and cut in half lengthwise. Slice thinly (about 3 mm thick).

Peel zucchini , leaving alternate strips of green. Slice thinly.

Wash cabbage and remove core. Cut into 3 cm strips.

Wash celery. Remove leaves, chop them coarsely and keep aside. Cut celery stalks into 5 mm pieces.

Prepare prawns and pork as for Fried Bean Sprouts With Pork and Prawns on p. 19.

Heat oil in large frying pan. Add onion and garlic. Stir-fry for 2 minutes until onion turns translucent. Add meat and prawns. Stir-fry for 5 minutes until cooked. Add fish sauce and vegetables. Stir-fry for 3 minutes until zucchini turns transparent. Add celery leaves. Mix well for 1 minute.

Sprinkle with pepper, spring onion and coriander leaves before serving. Serve hot.

FRIED BEAN SPROUTS WITH MUSSELS

NGHIEU XAO GIA

	20 mussels
500 g	bean sprouts
	1 onion
	1 clove garlic
2 Tbsps	oil
1 Tbsp	fish sauce
1 Tbsp	chopped spring onion
	1 handful coriander leaves
½ Tsp	pepper

Soak mussels in fresh water for 15 minutes. Discard any mussels which have open shells. Scrape mussel shells clean with a knife. Wash thoroughly under a tap. Open mussels with an oyster knife or a strong short knife. Remove flesh and pour liquid from inside the mussels into a small jar.

Wash bean sprouts and let dry in a colander.

Cut onion into 1 cm wedges and crush garlic.

Heat oil in large frying pan over fairly high heat. Add onion and garlic with a dash of salt. Stir-fry until onion turns translucent. Add mussels and liquid. Stir-fry for 5 minutes until cooked. Add fish sauce and pepper. Stir well and add bean sprouts. Stir-fry for 2–3 minutes until bean sprouts become slightly limp. Do not overcook.

Sprinkle with spring onion, coriander leaves and pepper before serving. Serve hot.

Vegetables

STUFFED CUCUMBER

DUA LEO DON THIT

	2 large cucumbers

Filling:

100 g	shelled raw prawns
300 g	minced pork
	1 large onion *(minced)*
1 Tsp	salt
1 Tsp	pepper
1 Tbsp	fish sauce
1 Tsp	monosodium glutamate *(optional)*

Soup:

3 L	water
	1 chicken soup cube
1 Tsp	chopped coriander leaves
1 Tbsp	chopped spring onion leaves
½ Tsp	pepper

Rub salt into prawns, then wash and dry them. Mince them very finely into a paste. Mix together onion, meat, prawns, fish sauce, salt, pepper and monosodium glutamate.

Cut off both ends of cucumber, and cut the remainder in half, making pieces of approximately 12 cm in length. Use the sharp point of a knife to remove pith and seeds. Stuff the hollow cucumber pieces with the filling. If there is any filling left over, roll it into balls of about 2 cm diameter (the size of a walnut).

Boil water in a saucepan. Add soup cube. Add cucumber and remaining filling. Boil for about 15 minutes, scooping off foam while boiling. Reduce heat and simmer for another 20 minutes. Test with skewer to see if cucumber is soft enough before removing from heat. Add coriander and spring onion leaves and pepper before serving.

Marrow or zucchini can be stuffed in the same way.

CHINESE TURNIP SALAD

GOI CU CAI

This is a similar salad to Jellyfish, Prawn and Pork Salad on p. 24. Replace carrots and cucumbers with 4 Chinese turnips and do not use jellyfish. Prepare the turnips in the same way as for carrots in the Jellyfish, Prawn and Pork salad recipe.

FRIED BITTER MELON

KHO HOA XAO

Follow ingredients and procedure as for Fried Zucchini With Pork and Prawns on p. 19, but replace zucchini with bitter melon. As bitter melon may take longer to cook, add ¼ cup water and cover for 5 minutes or so until cooked before adding egg.

PICKLED CHINESE TURNIPS

DUA CU CAI BOP XOI

	2 Chinese turnips
1¼ Tbsps	salt
1 Tbsp	white vinegar
½ cup	water
1 Tsp	sugar

Peel turnips and cut into thin slices. Mix with 1 tablespoon salt and leave for half an hour. Wash the turnip slices and squeeze out the water. Let dry in a colander.

Boil water, vinegar, sugar and remaining salt. Let the mixture cool and then pour over turnips.

Vegetables

STUFFED CABBAGE ROLLS IN SOUP

CAI BAP HAM THIT

300 g	cabbage leaves

Filling:

	1 medium onion *(minced)*
200 g	minced pork
½ Tsp	monosodium glutamate *(optional)*
1 Tbsp	fish sauce
½ Tsp	salt
½ Tsp	ground pepper

Soup:

2 L	water
	1 chicken soup cube
½ Tsp	pepper
1 Tsp	chopped coriander leaves
1 Tbsp	chopped spring onion leaves

Mix onion with meat and salt, pepper, fish sauce and monosodium glutamate.

Wash cabbage leaves. Cut out the middle rib and discard it. Cut each cabbage leaf into quarters large enough to wrap meat in. Blanch cabbage leaves for 1 minute, and then drain off.

Place meat filling on cabbage leaves and roll in the same way as for spring rolls (p. 34). Secure each roll with a toothpick or cotton.

Boil water in a saucepan. Add soup cube and cabbage rolls. Boil for 15 minutes, scooping off foam while boiling. Simmer for another 20 minutes. Remove from heat. Add coriander, spring onion leaves and pepper before serving.

FRIED SPINACH

RAU MUONG XAO

	1 bunch English spinach
150 g	fillet *or* rump steak
	1 medium-sized onion
1 Tsp	pepper
1½ Tbsps	fish sauce
1 Tbsp	cornflour
	1 large tomato
	1 clove garlic
3 Tbsps	oil

Cut fat off steak. Slice thinly (about 2 mm thick). Mince onion. Mix meat with onion, ½ teaspoon pepper, ½ tablespoon fish sauce and cornflour.

Wash spinach. Cut each stem into three. Slice tomato. Crush garlic.

Heat 1½ tablespoons oil in frying pan. Add garlic and stir-fry until fragrant. Add spinach; stir-fry for 3 minutes. Add remaining fish sauce and tomato. Stir-fry for 2 minutes. Remove onto plate.

Heat remaining oil in frying pan. Add meat and stir-fry for 5 minutes. Add 2 tablespoons water if meat sticks to pan. Remove meat from pan and place on top of spinach. Sprinkle with pepper. Serve hot.

PICKLED BEAN SPROUTS

DUA GIA XOI

100 g	bean sprouts
1 Tbsp	white vinegar
3 Tsps	sugar
½ Tsp	salt
1 × 3 cm	piece ginger *(sliced into matchsticks)*

Mix all ingredients together.

Vegetables

JELLYFISH, PRAWN AND PORK SALAD

GOI SUA

200 g	jellyfish
200 g	belly pork
200 g	prawns
	2 cucumbers
	2 carrots
	1 stalk celery with leaves
	mint leaves, chopped
	Vietnamese mint leaves, chopped
2 Tbsps	vinegar
3 Tbsps	sugar
1 Tbsp	fish sauce
	1 clove garlic
	juice of half lemon
	2 chillies *(optional)*
100 g	roasted peanuts, crushed

Soak jellyfish in water for a day. Wash well to get rid of salt. Cut into strips 7 cm long and 3 mm wide. Boil in water for 3 minutes and drain. Boil meat in 2 litres water for 20 minutes or until meat is cooked. Remove it from water. If prawns are not already cooked, boil prawns in same water. After they float to the surface, keep boiling for another 2 minutes. Drain prawns and let them cool, then shell them and cut the big ones in half.

Slice meat thinly (2–3 mm thick).

Peel and cut cucumbers into halves lengthwise. Remove pith and seeds. Cut each piece in half again lengthwise. Cut carrots in halves lengthwise, and then again. Slice carrots and cucumbers diagonally (2–3 mm wide and 5 cm long strips). Mix carrots and cucumber with 2 tablespoons salt. Let them stand for 1 hour. Wash salt off and squeeze tightly to get rid of water.

Slice celery diagonally (5 cm × 5 mm pieces). Chop celery leaves.

Mix all ingredients except for peanut and chillies. Remove seeds from chillies by making a cut lengthwise. Make 8 incisions along them, keeping the bottom stem part whole. Soak them in water to turn them into flowers.

Decorate top of salad with chilli flowers. Sprinkle with peanuts before serving.

This dish is eaten with prawn crackers and special fish sauce (see p. 89).

JELLY FISH, PRAWN AND PORK SALAD
(Goi Sua) opposite

STUFFED LEG OF PORK
(Gio Hen Don) recipe p. 27

Pork

Pork

GRILLED PORK BALLS

NEM NUONG

1 kg	leg *or* shoulder pork meat
100 g	pork fat *(optional)*
	6 cloves garlic, chopped
1 Tsp	salt
½ Tsp	baking powder
1 Tbsp	rum *or* anise
1 Tbsp	ground roasted rice *(see p. 9)*
3 Tbsps	sugar

Cut pork fat into matchstick strips and mix it with 2 tablespoons sugar. Let it stand for 1 hour.

Cut meat into 3 cm cubes and mix it with garlic, rum (or anisette), 1 teaspoon salt and 1 tablespoon sugar. Put mixture in a plastic bag, tie it, and put it in the freezer compartment of the refrigerator for 30 minutes. Turn the bag over every 10 minutes to stop meat hardening.

Take meat out of plastic bag and mince it very finely in a food processor, about 200 g at a time. When the meat changes to a pale whitish colour, remove it from the processor. Repeat the process until all the meat is finished. (Use a mortar and pestle if a food processor is not available.)

Mix the minced meat with baking powder, ground roasted rice and pork fat. After thorough mixing, roll mixture into balls about the size of a large cherry. Thread balls on skewers and grill over charcoal fire or under the griller if no charcoal is available.

These pork balls are served with a special bean sauce (see p. 42), rice paper, lettuce, cucumber and mint.

See p. 42 for the method of serving.

STUFFED LEG OF PORK

GIO HEO DON (GIO HEO BAC THAO)

	1 leg of pork *(about 1.5 kg)*
100 g	lean pork
100 g	belly pork *(without gristle or bone)*
3 Tsps	sugar
2 Tsps	salt
1 Tsp	ground pepper
1 Tsp	whole pepper
½ Tsp	potassium nitrate *(optional)*
1 Tbsp	anisette *or* sherry
	6 gloves garlic, crushed

Remove hair from leg and wash and dry it. With a sharp knife remove skin from leg, making sure the skin is in one piece. Then remove meat and fat from bone. Remove belly pork skin from meat. Boil belly pork skin until cooked. Slice boiled belly pork skin finely. Slice all meat and fat thinly (or mince it coarsely in the mincer). Mix meat with remaining ingredients and let the mixture stand for 15 minutes.

Sew the leg skin at the bottom, so as to make a pouch. Fill it with the meat and then sew the other end. Tie a piece of cheesecloth tightly around stuffed leg. Steam it in a steamer for about 2 hours. Test with a skewer to make sure the meat is cooked before removing it from the heat.

Let the meat cool down. Remove the cloth and replace it with aluminium foil. Refrigerate and use as cold meat.

This is a lovely dish for picnics or for lunch.

Pork

SHREDDED FRIED PORK

BI

500 g	leg pork *(without skin)*
100 g	shredded dried pork skin *(optional)*
1 Tsp	salt
1 Tbsp	anise *or* sherry
	3 cloves garlic
2 Tbsps	ground roasted rice *(thin)* *(see p. 9)*
1 Tsp	sugar

Wash and dry meat. Cut into 5 cm cubes. Rub in salt, anise (or sherry) and ½ crushed clove of garlic. Let meat stand for 1 hour. Fry over medium heat until golden and cooked. Do not overcook. Test with a skewer: it is done if no blood oozes out. Remove meat from heat and cut into matchstick pieces.

Soak skin in hot water for half an hour. Remove scum. Wash again three times in hot water. Boil water in large saucepan. Blanch skin for 1 minute. Rinse in cold water. Let drain in colander, then spread on tea towel to dry.

Mix meat and skin with crushed garlic, ground roasted rice, salt and sugar.

This dish is usually eaten with vermicelli or rice paper (see recipes on p. 29) and lemon and garlic fish sauce (p. 89).

GRILLED PORK CHOPS WITH CHILLIES AND LEMON GRASS

SUON UOP XA OT NUONG

To the ingredients for the recipe for Grilled Pork Chops With Garlic and Onion on p. 29, add 2 tablespoons chopped lemon grass and 1 teaspoon chopped chillies. Follow the same procedure.

STEWED LEG OF PORK IN FISH SAUCE

GIO HEO KHO

	1 leg of pork *(about 2 kg)*
1 Tsp	salt
2 Tbsps	sugar
1 Tbsp	caramel sauce *(see p. 89)*
4 Tbsps	fish sauce
1 Tsp	pepper

Wash pork leg thoroughly in warm water. Remove bone from leg (use bone for making stock). Cut meat together with skin into 3 cm cubes. Mix meat with salt, sugar, caramel sauce and fish sauce in a saucepan. Let it stand for 30 minutes.

Pour cold water into saucepan until the level is about 4 cm above the meat. Place saucepan over high heat and let the meat boil for 10 minutes, skimming off foam. Reduce heat and simmer for 1½ hours or until meat is tender.

Sprinkle with pepper before serving.

ROASTED PORK CHOPS

SUON HEO QUAY

600 g	forequarter pork chops
2 Tbsps	char siu powder
2 Tbsps	sugar
2 Tbsps	soya sauce
1 Tbsp	oil

Mix all ingredients together. Marinate the chops for 4 hours, turning occasionally.

Roast in a moderate oven for 1 hour. Chop pork into 3–4 cm cubes. Serve with rice and cucumber slices.

Pork

SHREDDED FRIED PORK ROLLED IN RICE PAPER

BI CUON

shredded fried pork (see recipe on p. 28)
rice papers
1 lettuce
mint leaves
lemon and garlic fish sauce (see p. 89)

Dip rice paper quickly in a large bowl of warm water. Make sure paper is wet right through but not soaking wet. Spread it out on a tea towel. Wet four pieces of rice paper in this way.

Wrap meat and vegetables in wet rice paper and fold it as indicated in the diagram below. Repeat process until meat is used up.

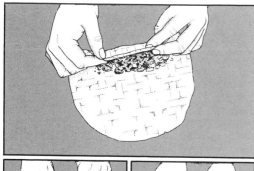

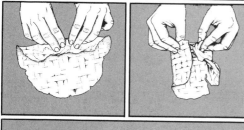

Serve roll with lemon and garlic fish sauce. Dip roll in sauce before eating.

GRILLED PORK CHOPS WITH GARLIC AND ONION

SUON UOP HANH TOI NUONG

½ Tsp	salt
1 Tbsp	sugar
2 Tbsps	fish sauce
	1 onion, minced
	4 cloves garlic, chopped
1 Tbsp	oil
600 g	pork chops

Mix all ingredients together and leave pork to marinate for 3–4 hours, turning meat occasionally.

Grill, or bake in moderate oven for 45–60 minutes. Chop into bite-sized pieces before serving.

SHREDDED FRIED PORK WITH NOODLES

BI BUN

shredded fried pork (see recipe on p. 28)
1 packet medium rice vermicelli (for 6 people)
200 g	bean sprouts
¼ lettuce, shredded
a few mint leaves

Boil water in a large saucepan. Drop dried noodles into boiling water and allow to boil for 5 minutes. Drain in a colander and rinse with cold water.

Blanch bean sprouts in boiling water for 1 minute and drain in a colander. Let them cool and then mix with shredded lettuce and mint leaves.

The pork is served with noodles, bean sprout salad and special lemon and garlic fish sauce (see recipe on p. 89).

Pork

MINCED PORK AND LEMON GRASS SAUSAGES

DOI

50 cm	sausage skin
350 g	minced pork
	1 onion, finely minced
	1 fresh lemon grass stalk *or* 1 tablespoon ground lemon grass
1 Tsp	ground pepper
1 Tsp	whole black pepper
1 Tbsp	sugar
1 Tbsp	fish sauce
½ Tsp	salt
¼ Tsp	monosodium glutamate *(optional)*
20 g	mung bean vermicelli
	7 cloud ear fungi

Mince about 10 cm of the bottom part of lemon grass finely (use chopper).

Soak vermicelli and fungi in hot water for 30 minutes. Drain vermicelli and fungi, and cut vermicelli into 4 cm lengths. Remove and discard hard core of fungus. Slice each fungus thinly into toothpick strips.

Mix all ingredients together. Stuff mixture into sausage skin. Tie both ends well.

Boil water in a large saucepan. Drop sausage in boiling water and boil for a further 15 minutes. Remove from water and prick sausage with sharp end of skewer thoroughly.

Grill over charcoal fire or under griller.

PORK LEG MEAT FRIED IN COCONUT AND TURMERIC

GIO HEO XAO LAN

1.5 kg	leg of pork
2 cups	coconut milk *(see p. 14)*
4 Tbsps	tinned coconut cream *or* first extract of coconut milk
2 Tbsps	finely chopped fresh lemon grass
1 Tbsp	turmeric
2 Tsps	bean sauce
½ Tsp	salt
⅔ Tbsp	sugar
	1 large onion
	4 cloves garlic
2 Tbsps	oil
50 g	roasted peanuts, crushed

Sauce:

1 Tbsp	fish sauce
½ Tsp	sugar
1 Tsp	lemon juice
½ Tsp	finely chopped fresh lemon grass
1 Tbsp	first extract coconut milk

Wash leg of pork thoroughly. Grill leg until skin turns golden brown. Remove bone and cut meat into bite-sized pieces (3 cm cubes).

Cut onion in half lengthwise and cut each half lengthwise into 6 sections. Slice garlic.

Heat oil in frying pan over moderately high heat. Add garlic and onion and stir-fry until onion turns translucent. Add meat, turmeric, lemon grass, bean sauce, salt and sugar. Stir-fry until meat changes colour. Add coconut milk. Reduce heat and simmer for 1 hour or until meat is tender. Remove from heat and add tinned coconut cream immediately.

Mix all sauce ingredients together.

Sprinkle with crushed peanuts before serving, and serve with the special sauce.

Pork

SWEET AND SOUR PORK CHOPS

SUON HEO XAO GIAM

1 kg	forequarter pork chops
½ Tsp	salt
	oil for deep frying

Batter:

¾ cup	wheat flour
6½ Tbsps	tapioca flour *or* cornflour
1 Tbsp	rice flour
¼ Tsp	salt
¼ Tsp	sugar
1 Tsp	baking powder
⅔ cup	cold water
1 Tbsp	oil

Sauce:

	½ cucumber
	1 carrot
100 g	cauliflower *or* broccoli *or* cabbage
	1 medium onion
	4 cloves garlic, crushed
	1 × 4 cm piece ginger
	5 pickled leeks *or* pickled onions
2 Tbsps	vinegar
2 Tbsps	sugar
½ Tsp	salt
1 Tbsp	soya sauce
1 Tbsp	oyster sauce
2 Tbsps	tomato paste
2 Tbsps	cornflour, mixed with ½ cup water
1 Tsp	sesame oil

Remove skin and fat from chops. Chop into 3 cm wide pieces (cut across bone). Sprinkle with salt.

Batter:
Sift all dry ingredients. Pour water slowly into mixture and stir well with a fork. Finally add oil to mixture. Prepare batter 4 hours before using, to enable baking powder to raise flour.

Sauce:
Cut cucumber in half lengthwise. Scoop out seeds and pith and cut in half again lengthwise. Cut carrot into quarters lengthwise. Now thinly slice cucumber and carrot diagonally. Rub in 1 table-spoon salt and let stand for 1 hour. Then squeeze out all the water and drain well.

Cut cauliflower into bite-sized pieces. Cut onion in half lengthwise and then cut each half into 6 sections. Cut ginger into matchstick strips. Cut leeks into 4 or 6, depending on size.

Mix vinegar, sugar, salt, soya sauce, oyster sauce and tomato paste.

Heat two tablespoons oil in frying pan over fairly high heat. Add onion and garlic and stir-fry until onion turns translucent. Add other vegetables and stir-fry for 2 minutes. Add vinegar mixture and mix well. Add cornflour and sesame oil. Mix well until sauce thickens.

Deep frying:
Heat enough oil for deep frying over moderate heat.

Dip pork pieces in batter and then drop them in the hot oil. Fry for about 10 minutes or until cooked.

Place chops on serving plate and pour pre-heated sauce over them. Serve with pepper and coriander leaves sprinkled on top.

Pork

PORK STEWED IN FISH SAUCE

THIT HEO KHO TAU

600 g	belly pork *or* leg pork
100 g	sugar
4 Tbsps	fish sauce
½ Tsp	salt
1 Tsp	caramel sauce *(for colouring)*
	4 boiled eggs *(optional)*
1 L	water

Wash meat and cut into 3–4 cm cubes. Boil water with sugar and caramel sauce and add pork. Skim occasionally. Boil pork for half an hour, then add fish sauce and salt and boil on high heat for 10 minutes. Skim off foam. Lower heat and simmer until meat is tender (about 1 hour). If water evaporates before meat is tender, add enough water to cover it and continue simmering until tender.

Shell eggs and add to meat twenty minutes before finishing time.

PIG'S HEAD PÂTÉ

CHA DAU HEO

	1 pig's head
⅓ Tsp	potassium nitrate
2 Tbsps	anisette *or* sherry
1 Tsp	salt
3 Tbsps	sugar
1 Tbsp	whole pepper

Remove hair from head and wash and dry thoroughly. Remove and discard any bones. Slice head thinly or mince coarsely in mincer. Mix meat with remaining ingredients, and marinate for 1 hour.

Pack mixture in small ovenproof dish, cover with cheesecloth and steam for 2 hours.

Chill pâté thoroughly in refrigerator before serving.

PORK FRIED IN FISH SAUCE

THIT HEO XAO MAN

600 g	lean belly pork *or* pork chops
	1 large onion *(sliced lengthwise)*
	4 cloves garlic *(sliced)*
3 Tbsps	fish sauce
1½ Tbsps	sugar
2 Tbsps	oil
½ Tsp	caramel sauce *(for colouring)*
1 Tsp	pepper
½ cup	water

Cut pork into 3 cm cubes.

Put oil in frying pan over medium heat. Fry garlic and onion until onion turns translucent. Add pork and stir over heat. When pork changes colour, add remaining ingredients except water. Mix well for 5 minutes. Then add water and reduce heat. Simmer over medium heat for 20 minutes until meat is cooked. (If water evaporates before meat is cooked add ¼ cup extra.)

Remove from heat and sprinkle with freshly-ground pepper.

ROAST PORK FILLET, CHINESE STYLE

XA XIU

600 g	pork fillets *(4 cm wide strips)*
4 Tsps	char siu powder
2 Tbsps	soya sauce
2 Tbsps	sugar
½ Tsp	monosodium glutamate *(optional)*
2 Tbsps	oil

Mix all ingredients together and marinate meat for 3–4 hours, turning meat occasionally.

Grill over charcoal fire or under griller.

Slice meat thinly before serving.

Pork

PRAWN AND PORK MEATLOAF

CHA HEO NUONG

250 g	dried prawns
500 g	lean pork
½ Tsp	salt
4 Tbsps	oil
	1 large onion
	10 eggs
1 Tsp	pepper
2 Tsps	sugar
½ Tsp	monosodium glutamate *(optional)*
2 Tsps	fish sauce

Soak prawns in warm water for half an hour, then wash and let drip-dry.

Wash meat and rub in salt. Fry meat in 2 tablespoons oil until golden and cooked. Mince meat together with prawns in food processor until fine.

Mince onion. Mix onion and remaining ingredients, keeping aside 3 egg yolks, with meat and prawns. Put mixture into a greased ovenproof dish. Bake in a moderately hot oven (180°C/350°F) for 30 minutes. When meat is cooked, spread the three egg yolks on top of the mixture and put it back in oven for another 10 minutes, or until egg yolks are cooked.

TONGUE STEWED WITH PEAS

LUOI HEO NAU DAU

	2 pig's tongues *or* 1 ox tongue
½ Tsp	salt
½ Tsp	pepper
1 Tbsp	cornflour
3 Tbsps	oil
	4 cloves garlic, sliced
	1 large onion, cut into 10 wedges
	2 carrots, diced
⅔ cup	tomato paste
300 g	frozen peas

Wash tongues and boil over medium heat, allowing 20 minutes per 500 g. Remove tongues from water, peel and cut into 4 cm cubes. Let them cool and then rub in salt, pepper and cornflour. Let stand for 1 hour.

Heat oil in casserole over fairly high heat. Add garlic and then onion and stir-fry until onion turns translucent. Add tongues and stir-fry for 2 minutes. Add carrots and stir-fry for 2 minutes. Add tomato paste and enough water to cover meat. Reduce heat and simmer until meat is tender. Add peas. Cook for another 10 minutes.

Pork

SPRING ROLLS

CHA GIO

200 g	minced pork
200 g	crabmeat
30 g	mung bean vermicelli
	10 cloud ear fungi
	10 Chinese dried mushrooms
	1 medium carrot (shredded)
	2 medium onions (minced)
½ Tsp	salt
1 Tsp	fish sauce
2 Tsps	sugar
½ Tsp	pepper
½ Tsp	monosodium glutamate (optional)
	spring roll skins or rice papers

Filling:

Soak vermicelli in hot water for 10 minutes, then drain and cut into lengths of 7–8 cm.

Soak cloud ear fungi in hot water for 20 minutes. Wash and drain. Discard the hard parts and chop finely.

Soak Chinese mushrooms in hot water for 30 minutes. Wash and drain and remove hard stems. Slice mushrooms into matchsticks. To make mushrooms more crunchy, the following optional procedure can be followed. After discarding the stems, boil the mushrooms in water with ½ teaspoon salt for 5 minutes. Heat 2 tablespoons oil in a frying pan and fry the mushrooms with a teaspoon of sugar for 5 minutes. Then remove from heat and slice them into matchsticks.

Mix all the ingredients together. They can then be rolled in either Chinese spring roll skins or Vietnamese rice papers, as follows:

Spring roll skins:

Ready-made spring roll skins are readily available from Chinese grocery stores. If possible, buy the small ones of about 12 cm square. If these are not available then buy the large skins and cut each one into four. Unlike Chinese spring rolls, Vietnamese spring rolls are of small size.

First, fold skin down as shown in Fig. 1. Place enough filling on to folded skin. Fold in the two ends, then roll up. Seal each roll with a paste made from a little flour and water mixed together. This is the best method to use, as it will stop the skins tearing.

Rice papers:

If possible obtain the small rice papers: otherwise divide each large one into four.

Mix two tablespoons of white vinegar, 1 teaspoon sugar with ¾ soup bowl of warm water. Rub both sides of rice paper with water mixture and spread it on a tea-towel. Repeat this procedure 4 times. Make sure paper is pliable before proceeding to next step.

Fill the rice papers as described above.

Repeat procedure until meat filling is used up.

Deep-fry rolls in plenty of hot oil over medium heat.

Drain in a colander. Serve with lettuce, mint, and lemon and garlic fish sauce (see p. 89) and boiled rice vermicelli (see p. 29).

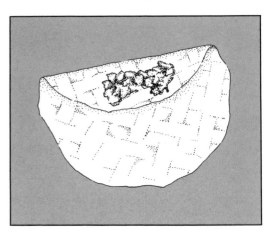

Pork

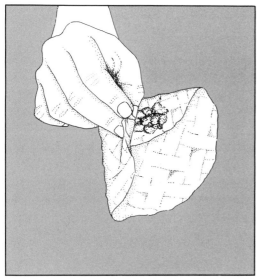

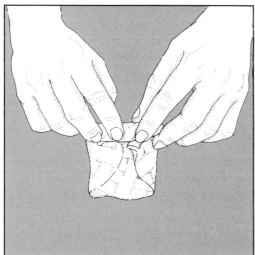

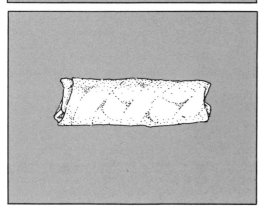

ROAST BELLY PORK, CHINESE STYLE

THIT HEO QUAY

600 g	belly pork *(in one piece)*
4 Tsps	char siu powder
2 Tbsps	soya sauce
2 Tbsps	sugar
½ Tsp	monosodium glutamate *(optional)*

Wash pork thoroughly and dry well with paper towels or cloth. Place meat on a plate with skin side up. Cover skin with a 5 mm layer of salt. Let stand in refrigerator for 6 hours.

Remove meat from refrigerator and wash it under running water. Dry thoroughly with cloth or paper towels. Mix remaining ingredients with pork. Marinate for 3 hours, turning meat occasionally.

Place meat on a rack, skin side up, in roasting pan. Put in a hot oven (200°C/400°F) for 30 minutes, then reduce heat to moderate (180°C/350°F) and continue roasting for another 40 minutes. Do not baste meat.

Chop pork into 3–4 cm cubes. Serve with rice and cucumber slices or with fine rice vermicelli, lettuce, cucumber and special lemon and garlic fish sauce (see p. 89).

Pork

PRAWNS AND LEG OF PORK SOUP WITH VERMICELLI

SUONG GIO HEO

Soup:

	1 leg of pork
3 L	water
1 Tsp	salt
1 Tbsp	fish sauce
	1 medium-sized onion *(minced)*
1 Tbsp	tomato puree

Prawn paste:

300 g	shelled raw prawns
	1 large onion
	white of 1 egg
¼ Tsp	salt
1 Tsp	sugar
¼ Tsp	monosodium glutamate *(optional)*
1 Tbsp	tapioca flour *or* cornflour

Garnish:

200 g	medium rice vermicelli
200 g	bean sprouts, blanched
	mint leaves, sliced
	a few lettuce leaves, sliced thinly
	hoisin sauce
	chopped peanuts
	chilli paste

Wash leg of pork thoroughly. Boil water in a large saucepan and add pork with a teaspoon of salt. Boil over medium heat for 20 minutes. Skim, reduce heat and boil for another hour or until meat is tender. Add fish sauce. Taste for seasoning. Add ½ teaspoon monosodium glutamate if desired.

Rub 1 tablespoon salt into prawns. Wash, and drain thoroughly on paper towels. Slice onion, and mince together with prawns into a fine paste. Beat white of egg until stiff. Mix half of white of egg and remaining ingredients with prawn paste.

Remove leg of pork from soup and slice meat and skin fairly thinly.

Fry onion until slightly golden, and add to soup. Roll prawn paste into 5 mm thick strips and drop them into boiling soup.

To give colour to soup, add roe of prawns or, if roe is not available, add 1 tablespoon of tomato puree.

Drop vermicelli into boiling water and boil for 5 to 10 minutes, until soft. Drain in a colander and rinse with cold water. Let bean sprouts cool after blanching and mix them with mint and lettuce.

To serve:
Place vermicelli in individual bowls, together with a handful of bean sprouts, lettuce and meat. Pour soup with prawns on top, then sprinkle with chopped peanuts. Put hoisin sauce in small bowls and dip meat and prawns whenever needed.

Fish & Seafood

Fish & Seafood

PRAWNS AND PORK ROLLED IN RICE PAPER

GOI CUON

500 g	raw prawns *or* cooked prawns *(small to medium)*
300 g	belly pork *(without skin)*
	20 rice papers *(medium to large)*
	1 lettuce
	some mint leaves
30 g	fresh bean sprouts
100 g	medium rice vermicelli
	1 bunch *he (optional)*

Soya bean and peanut sauce
Tuong:

	4 cloves garlic
1 Tbsp	oil
½ cup	refined bean sauce
½ Tbsp	fish sauce
2 Tbsps	vinegar
3 Tbsps	sugar
1 Tbsp	peanut butter
1 cup	water
30 g	roasted peanuts, crushed

Wash pork thoroughly. Boil 2 litres of water in saucepan, add salt and meat. Boil over moderate heat for 20 minutes or until meat is cooked. Remove meat from water.

If prawns are uncooked add to boiling water. After they float to the surface, keep boiling for another 2 minutes. Then drain and let them cool. When cool, shell prawns and slice the big ones into halves.

Place vermicelli in boiling water and boil for 5 to 10 minutes until soft. Wash in cold water and drain in colander.

Slice meat thinly (2–3 mm thickness).

Wet rice papers.

Place rice paper on plate and put on it ingredients in the following order: lettuce leaf, 2 or 3 mint leaves, bean sprouts, vermicelli and about 4 meat slices.

Fold in the two sides and roll paper up once. Place 2–3 prawns on unrolled paper, roll up once more. Then add one *he* stalk, letting its end poke out of roll end. Finish rolling up.

It is important to follow this procedure to avoid any tearing of the paper and for aesthetic reasons. The different colours of the ingredients will show through the paper.

Repeat the process until all ingredients are used up. If you find this too time-consuming, you can place all ingredients on the table and then show your guests how to make their own rolls.

To make sauce, first chop garlic finely. Heat oil over moderate heat and add garlic. Stir-fry until garlic turns slightly golden. Add bean sauce, fish sauce, vinegar, sugar, peanut butter and water. Stir well over heat until sugar has melted. This sauce should taste slightly sweet and should not be too thick. Pour into a small serving bowl and sprinkle crushed peanuts on top.

How to serve:
Pour sauce in individual sauce bowls with a dash of chilli sauce if required, and dip roll in sauce.

PRAWNS FRIED IN BUTTER

TOM RIEM BEURRE

500 g	raw prawns
½ Tsp	salt
2 Tsps	sugar
30 g	butter
	5 cloves garlic, finely chopped
1 Tbsp	oil

Prepare prawns as on p. 12. Heat oil in frying pan over moderate heat. Add garlic and stir-fry until fragrant. Add prawns and seasonings and stir-fry for 1 minute. Reduce heat.

Cook over low heat until most of the liquid has evaporated. Stir occasionally. Add butter before removing from heat.

Serve with a dash of pepper.

Fish & Seafood

STUFFED CRAB SHELLS

CUA DON MAI CHIEN

	2 medium-sized crabs
200 g	minced pork
30 g	mung bean vermicelli
10 g	cloud ear fungus
	1 large onion, finely minced
	5 eggs
½ Tsp	salt
1 Tbsp	fish sauce
1 Tsp	sugar
1 Tsp	pepper
2 Tbsps	oil

If crabs are not already cooked, kill and wash as described in the recipe for Crab Fried in Salt on p. 50. Then cook meat as shown on page 50.

Remove shells from crabs, making sure the shells are clean and whole. Pull off crab meat and shred finely.

Soak vermicelli in warm water for 10 minutes. Soak fungus in hot water for 20 minutes. Drain vermicelli and cut into 3 cm strips. Drain fungus, discard core and slice fungus finely into strips as thin as toothpicks.

Separate one egg and keep yolk aside.

Mix all ingredients together except for the egg yolk. Wash shells and dry them, and oil the insides. Then fill them with mixture.

Bake in moderate oven (180°C/350°F) for 30 minutes, or fry in oil in frying pan.

After the stuffing is cooked, brush egg yolk on top for nice colour presentation.

SWEET AND SOUR SQUIDS

MUC XAO GIAM

400 g	squid
	2 cucumbers
	2 tomatoes
	1 large onion
	3 cloves garlic
2 Tbsps	oil
2 Tbsps	vinegar
1 Tbsp	sugar
½ Tsp	salt
2 Tbsps	soya sauce
	2 celery tops, sliced
2 Tbsps	cornflour mixed with ½ cup water
	coriander leaves
½ Tsp	pepper

Prepare squids as described on p. 12.

Make criss-cross cuts on the inside of squids, about 5 mm apart. Cut squids into 5 × 3 cm pieces. (This is partly for aesthetic reasons and partly to tenderise the squid meat.)

Cut cucumber in half lengthwise. Remove and discard seeds and pith. Cut each half into halves again, lengthwise. Now cut each piece into 5 cm × 5 mm pieces. Mix cucumber with 1 tablespoon salt and let stand for half an hour. Mix well again and squeeze out all the water. Wash in cold water once to rinse the salt out, and squeeze out the water again.

Cut tomatoes in half, then into 1.5 cm wide sections. Do likewise with onion. Slice garlic.

Heat oil in frying pan over moderately high heat. Add garlic and then onion and stir-fry until onion turns translucent. Add squids and stir-fry for 2 minutes. Add tomatoes and stir-fry for half a minute. Add seasonings and then cucumber and celery tops. Stir-fry for half a minute. Add cornflour and stir until sauce thickens. Sprinkle with coriander leaves and pepper before serving.

STUFFED CRAB SHELLS
(Cua Don Mai Chien) opposite

SWEET AND SOUR FISH
(Ca Chien Sauce Chua Ngot) opposite

Fish & Seafood

SWEET AND SOUR FISH

CA CHIEN SAUCE CHUA NGOT

1 kg	whole fish *(firm-fleshed)*
	1 egg
6 Tbsps	wheat flour
¼ Tsp	salt
2 Tbsps	oil

Sauce:

	1 medium onion
	3 cloves garlic
	1 leek
1 × 4 cm	piece of ginger
	1 small carrot
	½ capsicum (red or green pepper)
	1 tomato, peeled
	5 pickled leeks *or* small pickled onions
2 Tbsps	oil
1 Tbsp	oyster sauce
1 Tsp	sesame oil
2 Tbsps	vinegar
2 Tbsps	sugar
1 Tbsp	soya sauce
2 Tbsps	cornflour, mixed with ½ cup water

Wash and scale fish and make a diagonal incision in it. Dry fish with cloth or paper towels. Rub salt into fish.

Beat egg until stiff. Place flour on large plate. Just before frying, brush both sides of fish with egg and then roll fish in flour. Drop fish immediately into hot oil. Fry on both sides over medium heat until golden brown.

To make sauce, chop onion, garlic, leek, ginger, carrot, capsicum, tomato and pickled leeks finely. Keep each type of vegetable apart from the others.

Heat oil in saucepan over moderately high heat. Fry onion and garlic until onion turns translucent. Add leek, ginger and carrot and stir-fry for 1 minute. Add capsicum, tomato and pickled leeks and stir-fry for 1 minute. Add remaining ingredients except cornflour and stir-fry until sauce starts bubbling. Add cornflour and stir well until sauce thickens.

Place fish on a bed of lettuce or watercress. Pour heated sweet and sour sauce over fish before serving.

FRIED WHOLE FISH WITH LEMON AND GARLIC FISH SAUCE

CA CHIEN DAM NUOC MAM OT

1 kg	whole fish *(firm-fleshed)*
	2 cloves garlic
2 Tbsps	oil
	lemon and garlic fish sauce *(see p. 89)*

Wash and scale fish. Dry with cloth or paper towels. Make diagonal incision into thickest part of fish on both sides.

Heat oil in frying pan (preferably a non-stick frying pan) over moderate heat. Add garlic and then fish. Fry on both sides until fish is golden brown and cooked.

Place fish on a large plate. Sprinkle ⅓ cup lemon and garlic fish sauce over it.

Fish & Seafood

PRAWN BALLS ON SKEWERS

CHAO TOM

500 g	shelled raw prawns
100 g	pork fat
½ Tsp	salt
1 Tbsp	sugar
	1 egg white
1 Tsp	cornflour
	6 cloves garlic
	a few sticks of peeled sugar cane (optional)
	mung bean and soya bean sauce

Mung bean and soya bean sauce

100 g	shelled mung beans or yellow split peas
½ cup	water
½ cup	refined bean sauce
	1 clove garlic
1 Tbsp	oil
2 Tbsps	sugar
2 Tbsps	vinegar
1 Tsp	good quality fish sauce
50 g	chopped roasted peanuts

Devein prawns. Rub 1 heaped teaspoon salt into them, mix well and then wash with cold water until no more foam appears. Dry well with cloth or paper towels. Keep in refrigerator.

Cut pork fat into matchstick strips, mix them with ⅔ tablespoon sugar, and leave for 30 minutes.

Chop garlic and mix it with the prawns. Beat egg white until stiff. Mince prawns and garlic finely in food processor. Add salt and sugar and continue mincing for 1 minute. Add cornflour and just a bit over half of the beaten egg white. Mix well. Form the mixture into balls about the size of small plums. Thread prawn balls on to skewers or wrap them around sugar cane if available.

Grill under griller or over charcoal fire. Serve hot.

To make sauce, cook mung beans or split peas in 2 cups water until soft. Put peas in food processor to mince into a fine paste. Chop garlic. Heat oil over moderate heat in a saucepan, add garlic. Fry until slightly golden, then add bean sauce and pea mixture. Mix well. Add vinegar, sugar, ½ cup water, fish sauce and mix well. This sauce should be slightly sweet and not too thin or thick. Sprinkle peanuts on top of sauce before serving. (If it is too thick add more water and stir well over moderate heat.)

How to serve:

You will need some rice papers that have previously been wetted with warm water, some lettuce, cucumber slices and mint leaves. Place these items on separate plates and then on the table.

Pour the sauce into individual small bowls.

Each person is supposed to make his or her own roll. Place one or two pieces of rice paper on a plate. Put lettuce, cucumber and mint on rice paper. Finally, place one or two prawn balls on top. Tuck in the ends of the rice paper like an envelope and roll it up. Dip roll in bowl of bean sauce. A dash of chilli sauce in the bean sauce would give a lift to the flavour.

Fish & Seafood

STEAMED MINCED PRAWNS

CHA TOM HAP

600 g	shelled raw prawns
1 Tsp	salt
100 g	pork fat
1 Tbsp	sugar
	1 medium onion *or* 5 shallots
1 Tsp	cornflour
	2 eggs

Prepare prawns as on p. 12. Dry prawns with cloth or paper towels.

Boil fat until cooked and then cut into matchstick strips. Mix fat strips with 1 tablespoon sugar and let stand (in sun, if possible) for 30 minutes. Mince onion and prawns together finely. Add salt and cornflour and mix well.

Separate yolks from whites of eggs. Beat egg whites until stiff. Mix whites with pork fat and prawn mixture.

Put hot water in bottom of steamer. Spread a sheet of aluminium foil on top part of steamer. Oil the aluminium sheet and then make some holes in it. Place prawn mixture on top of aluminium sheet, and spread it out with the flat part of a knife that has been oiled, to a thickness of 3 cm. Cover with lid and steam for 30 minutes or until cooked.

Meanwhile, beat the yolks of the eggs. When prawn mixture is cooked, spread egg yolk on top of it. Leave steamer uncovered and continue steaming for a few minutes until the egg yolks are cooked.

Cut steamed prawn mixture into 3 cm diamond shapes. Arrange on a plate in the shape of a flower.

GRILLED FISH WITH PORK AND RICE PAPER

CA NUONG THIT LUOT

	1 large bream *(1.5 kg)*
300 g	belly pork
	20 pieces rice paper
	1 small cucumber
	1 small lettuce
	some mint leaves
½ cup	chopped spring onions
3 Tbsps	oil
	soya bean and peanut sauce *(see p. 39)*

There are two ways of cooking the fish.
1 Wash fish, leaving scales on. Grill fish on a charcoal fire until cooked. Do not overcook. Before serving, remove skin and scales from fish.
2 Wash and scale fish. Wrap in aluminium foil and bake fish in oven until cooked.

Boil 1 litre water in saucepan. Add pork and boil it over moderate heat until cooked. Slice meat thinly.

Heat oil in saucepan. Fry spring onions for 1 minute. Pour this mixture on top of fish before serving.

Wash lettuce and cucumber. Slice cucumber thinly. Arrange it, with lettuce leaves and mint leaves, on a large plate.

Wet rice paper.

How to serve:
Place vegetables, fish, meat and sauce on the table. Pour sauce into individual bowls. Each person makes his/her own roll with a piece of rice paper, some fish, meat slices and vegetables. Then dip roll in bean sauce before eating.

A dash of chilli paste in the sauce would give a lift to the flavour.

Fish & Seafood

CRAB CLAWS WRAPPED IN PRAWN PASTE

CANG CUA CHIEN TOM

	24 crab claws
200 g	shelled raw prawns
	1 egg white
¼ Tsp	salt
½ Tsp	sugar
	2 small onions
½ Tsp	cornflour
	oil for deep frying

Sauce:

	2 cloves garlic
	1 large onion
	10 pickled Chinese leeks or 5 pickled onions
1 × 4 cm	piece of ginger
1 Tbsp	oil
¼ Tsp	salt
1 Tbsp	soya sauce
1 Tbsp	oyster sauce
2 Tbsps	vinegar
3½ Tbsps	sugar
½ cup	water
1 Tsp	sesame oil
2 Tbsps	cornflour blended in ¼ cup water

Detach crab claws and wash thoroughly. Steam them in steamer for 10 minutes. Crack claws carefully so as to preserve the ends.

Prepare prawns as described on p. 12. Dry them with cloth or paper towels.

Beat egg white until stiff. Slice onions thinly. Place prawns and onions in food processor and mince for 2 minutes. Add salt and sugar and mince for 2 more minutes. Add 2 tablespoons egg white and mince for another minute. Add cornflour and mince for another minute (it should be a fine paste).

Wrap prawn mixture around crab claws, leaving end claws unwrapped. Deep fry in oil until golden brown. Serve on top of a bed of watercress or lettuce, to be eaten with sauce.

To make sauce, chop garlic, onion, leeks and ginger separately. Heat oil over moderate heat. Add garlic and stir-fry until fragrant. Add onion, leeks and ginger and stir-fry until onion turns translucent. Add salt, soya sauce, oyster sauce, vinegar, sugar and water. Boil gently for 10 minutes. Add sesame oil. Test seasonings. Pour in cornflour and stir continuously until sauce thickens.

Use the crab meat from the rest of the crab for another dish.

PRAWNS FRIED IN FISH SAUCE

TOM RIEM NUOC MAM

500 g	raw prawns
¼ Tsp	salt
	4 cloves garlic
	1 medium onion
⅔ Tbsp	oil
2 Tbsps	fish sauce
1 Tbsp	sugar

Shell and devein prawns. Rub in salt for a few minutes. Rinse with cold water until no more foam appears and then drain in a colander.

Chop garlic finely. Cut onion lengthwise into 5 mm strips.

Heat oil in frying pan over moderate heat. Add garlic and onion and stir-fry until onion turns translucent. Add prawns and stir-fry for 3–5 minutes or until prawns are cooked. Add seasonings. Reduce heat and stir-fry for a few minutes until most of the liquid has evaporated.

Sprinkle some pepper on top of prawns before serving.

Fish & Seafood

FISH AND TOMATO SOUP WITH VERMICELLI

CA NAU SUN

2 L	water
1 kg	fish (preferably mullet)
½ Tsp	salt
50 g	tamarind (this is important to the flavour of this soup. However, if it is not available, it can be replaced by juice of half a lemon.)
1 Tbsp	fish sauce
2 Tbsps	sugar
2 Tbsps	oil
	3 cloves garlic, finely chopped
	1 large onion, sliced thinly
2 Tbsps	finely chopped lemon grass
	3 ripe tomatoes, cut in quarters
2 Tbsps	bean sauce
	some basil, finely chopped
50 g	roasted peanuts, crushed

Garnish:

100 g	medium rice vermicelli
200 g	bean sprouts (see p. 23)
3 Tbsps	hoisin sauce

Boil 2 litres water in saucepan. Add salt and fish and boil gently over medium heat until fish is cooked. Remove it from stock and put aside on a plate.

Add tamarind to stock and boil for 5 minutes. Remove tamarind. Add fish sauce and sugar to stock and stir well. Remove saucepan from stove.

Remove bones from fish. Shred fish into big pieces (about 3 cm wide).

Heat oil in a large frying pan over medium heat. Add garlic and onion and stir-fry until onion turns translucent. Add lemon grass and stir-fry for a few seconds. Add fish and stir-fry for a few seconds. Add tomatoes and bean sauce and stir-fry gently for 2 minutes. Make sure not to break the fish pieces.

Return stock to stove, and bring to boil. Add fish mixture to stock and stir well. Boil gently for 2 minutes. Place vermicelli in boiling water, boil for 5 to 10 minutes until soft, rinse in cold water and drain in colander. Blanch bean sprouts in boiling water and drain.

Sprinkle basil and peanuts on top of soup before serving.

How to serve:

In each individual bowl, place about 2 tablespoons vermicelli and 2 tablespoons bean sprouts. Pour fish and stock over contents. Put hoisin sauce in individual sauce-bowls and dip fish in sauce if required.

A dash of chilli paste and a few drops of fish sauce would give a lift to the flavour.

FRIED FISH IN BUTTER

CA MUOI CHIEN BEURRE

1 kg	whole fish (firm-fleshed)
½ Tsp	salt
1 Tsp	pepper
1 Tbsp	flour
2 Tbsps	oil
2 Tbsps	melted butter
20 g	chopped almonds, peanuts or cashew nuts

Prepare fish as in Fried Whole Fish With Lemon and Garlic Fish Sauce, on p. 41.

Rub salt and pepper into fish, and let stand for 1 hour. Sprinkle flour on both sides of fish. Heat oil in frying pan (preferably non-stick frying pan) over moderate heat. Fry fish on both sides until golden brown and cooked. Remove on to a preheated plate. Pour melted butter on to both sides of fish.

Sprinkle nuts on top of fish before serving.

Fish & Seafood

FISH AND PORK LEG RICE PORRIDGE

CHAO CA GIO HEO

	1 small leg of pork *(1 kg)*
3 L	water
½ Tsp	salt
	1 medium-sized mullet *or* bream
1 cup	rice
3 Tbsps	oil
	1 large onion, thinly sliced
1½ Tbsps	fish sauce
¼ Tsp	monosodium glutamate *(optional)*
2 Tbsps	chopped spring onions
2 Tbsps	coriander leaves
1 Tsp	pepper

Garnish:

100 g	medium rice vermicelli
200 g	bean sprouts, blanched for 2 minutes
2 Tbsps	chopped mint leaves
100 g	roasted peanuts, crushed
3 Tbsps	hoisin sauce

Wash leg of pork well. Boil water in large saucepan. Add ½ teaspoon salt and leg of pork, and boil over moderate to high heat for 10 minutes. Skim continuously. Reduce heat to medium. Add fish and boil gently for about 15 minutes. Remove fish from stock when cooked. Continue cooking pork until tender (about 1 hour), then remove pork from stock.

While meat is cooking, wash rice and let it drain well. Heat 1 tablespoon oil in frying pan, and fry rice over medium heat for 2–3 minutes. Add rice to stock, and simmer for about 1 hour.

Remove bones from fish and shred it into bite-sized pieces. Remove bone from pork and slice meat into bite-sized pieces.

Place vermicelli in boiling water, boil for 5 to 10 minutes until soft, rinse in cold water and drain in colander.

Heat 2 tablespoons of oil in frying pan over medium heat. Add onion and stir-fry until it is fragrant. Add fish, remaining salt, fish sauce, monosodium glutamate (if desired). Add fish and meat to rice porridge. Before serving, check the seasonings. Sprinkle with spring onions, coriander leaves and pepper before serving.

How to serve:
In each individual soup bowl, place ½ tablespoon vermicelli, 1 tablespoon bean sprouts and ½ teaspoon mint leaves. Pour rice soup over contents. Sprinkle with peanuts before eating.

A dash of hoisin sauce or fish sauce would give a lift to the flavour.

FRIED FISH IN LEMON GRASS

CA MUOI XA OT CHIEN

1 kg	whole fish *(firm-fleshed)*
½ Tsp	salt
1 Tbsp	chopped lemon grass
1 Tsp	chopped fresh chilli *or* ground chilli *(optional)*
2 Tbsps	oil

Prepare fish as in Fried Whole Fish With Lemon and Garlic Fish Sauce, on p. 41. Dry well. Rub salt, lemon grass and chilli into fish and let it stand for 1 hour, turning it over occasionally. Heat oil in frying pan (preferably non-stick pan) over moderate heat. Fry fish on both sides until golden brown and cooked.

Fish & Seafood

SLICED FISH AND RICE PORRIDGE

CHAO CA THAI

½ Tsp	salt
500 g	pork bones
1¼ cups	rice
1 Tbsp	fish sauce
¼ Tsp	monosodium glutamate (optional)
700 g	fish fillets (firm-fleshed)
1 × 5 cm	piece ginger
2 Tbsps	coarsely chopped spring onions
1 Tbsp	soya sauce
1 Tsp	pepper
½ cup	finely shredded lettuce
2 Tbsps	chopped coriander leaves

Boil 2.5 litres of water in saucepan over medium heat. Add salt and pork bones and boil for 10 minutes, skimming off foam. Reduce heat and simmer for 1½ hours. Remove bones from stock. Wash rice well and add it to stock. Simmer for 1 hour. Add fish sauce and monosodium glutamate. Add 1 cup hot water if porridge is too thick.

Slice fish fillets finely. Peel and cut ginger into matchstick strips. Place fish slices on a large plate. Sprinkle ginger, spring onions, soya sauce and pepper on top.

How to serve:
Pre-heat individual serving bowls. Place fish, ginger and spring onions in each bowl. Pour simmering rice porridge on top. Stir well so that fish gets cooked.

Sprinkle lettuce and chopped coriander leaves on top before serving. Add a few drops of soya sauce if required.

SOUR FISH SOUP

CA NAU CHUA

1 kg	whole fish (mullet or bream)
300 g	bean sprouts
	3 ripe tomatoes
	2 stalks bac ha or celery
20 g	tamarind or juice of half a small lemon
1.5 L	water
½ Tsp	salt
2 Tbsps	fish sauce
1 Tbsp	sugar
½ Tbsp	oil
	1 clove garlic, sliced
	handful of basil leaves
	coriander leaves

Wash and scale fish. Cut into 3 or 4 pieces according to size. Wash bean sprouts and drain. Cut tomatoes into 8–10 pieces lengthwise. Cut *bac ha* or celery into 2 cm thick pieces.

Soak tamarind in 2 tablespoons boiling water for half an hour.

Boil water in saucepan and add fish. Boil gently over moderate heat for half an hour. Remove fish from stock on to a plate. Add tamarind to stock and let it boil for 5 minutes. Remove tamarind from stock. Add seasonings: salt, fish sauce and sugar.

Heat oil in a small frying pan. Add garlic and fry until light gold. Just before serving, add fish and garlic to stock. When it starts boiling again, add vegetables and remove immediately from heat.

Chop herbs finely and sprinkle on top of soup before serving.

Fish & Seafood

FISH AND TOMATO SOUP

CA NAU NGOT

1 kg	whole fish (firm-fleshed)
	5 spring onions
	1 chilli (optional)
1.5 L	water
¼ Tsp	salt
2 Tbsps	fish sauce
1 Tbsp	sugar
	3 ripe tomatoes
	handful of coriander leaves
½ Tsp	pepper
	1 lemon

Wash and scale fish, and cut it into 3 or 4 pieces. Cut spring onions into 5 or 6 pieces. Slice chilli.

Boil water in saucepan on medium heat. Add salt, fish sauce and sugar. Add fish and boil for 10 minutes. Add tomatoes and boil for another 10 minutes. Remove from heat. Add spring onions, coriander leaves, pepper and chilli.

Squeeze juice of a lemon into soup before serving.

DEEP-FRIED PRAWN TOAST

BANH MI CHIEN TOM

300 g	shelled raw prawns
300 g	pork chop meat
	1 large onion
¼ Tsp	salt
1 Tbsp	fish sauce
1 Tsp	sugar
1 Tsp	pepper
50 g	wheat flour
1½ Tbsps	cornflour
½ Tsp	baking powder
4½ Tbsps	water
500 g	thin slices bread (2–3 days old), crusts removed
	oil for deep frying
	sesame seeds (optional)

Slice onion and meat and mince these two ingredients in food processor for 1 minute.

Prepare prawns as described on p. 12. Dry thoroughly with cloth. Place prawns on chopping board and flatten each with the flat part of the chopper.

Mix prawns and meat together. Place mixture in food processor and mince for another 2 minutes. Add salt, fish sauce, sugar and pepper. Mix well.

Mix flour and cornflour with baking powder and water. Brush both sides of bread slice with flour mixture thinly. (The purpose of using the flour mixture is to stop the bread from soaking up too much oil.) Spread a thin layer of prawn mixture on both sides of bread. Then coat with sesame seeds. Deep fry in hot oil. Drain in colander before serving.

Fish & Seafood

STUFFED SQUID

MUC ONG DON THIT CHIEN

400 g	squid *(about 9 cm long)*
4 Tbsps	oil

Filling:

200 g	minced pork
	1 onion, minced
½ Tsp	salt
½ Tsp	pepper
1 Tsp	fish sauce

Sauce:

1 Tbsp	oil
	2 cloves garlic, chopped
	1 onion, minced
	1 tomato, chopped
3 Tbsps	tomato paste, mixed with 1 Tbsp water
½ Tsp	salt
1 Tbsp	sugar
1 Tsp	soya sauce
1 Tsp	cornflour, mixed with 1 Tbsp water

Prepare squid as described on p. 12.

Mix pork with seasonings for filling. Stuff squids three-quarters full with pork mixture.

Heat oil over moderate heat. Fry squids on one side for about 5–8 minutes. Turn on the other side and fry for the same amount of time or until they are golden brown.

To make the sauce, heat oil over moderate heat. Add garlic and onion. Stir-fry until onion turns translucent. Add chopped tomato and stir-fry for 2 minutes. Add tomato paste and seasonings and stir well. Add cornflour if sauce is not thick enough.

Cut cooked squids into halves or 3 pieces and arrange on a serving plate. Just before serving, pour hot sauce over squids and sprinkle with pepper and coriander leaves.

CRAB AND SAGO SOUP

CUA NAU CANH BOT BANG

1.5 L	chicken stock
200 g	crab meat
½ cup	sago
2 Tbsps	fish sauce
¼ Tsp	monosodium glutamate *(optional)*
1 Tbsp	coriander leaves
¼ Tsp	pepper

Bring chicken stock to the boil. Wash and drain sago. Add to boiling stock and cook over a low heat, stirring continuously for 2–3 minutes or until sago turns completely transparent. Add crabmeat and seasoning. Sprinkle with coriander leaves before serving.

Fish & Seafood

SLICED FISH FRIED IN BEAN SAUCE

CA THAI XAO TUONG

700 g	fish fillets *(bream or mullet)*
1 × 4 cm	piece of ginger
	1 medium onion
	2 cloves garlic
2 Tbsps	oil
2 Tbsps	bean sauce
1 Tbsp	sugar
2 Tbsps	celery leaves, coarsely chopped
1 Tbsp	coriander leaves
¼ Tsp	pepper

Slice fish fillets thinly into 6 × 4 cm pieces. Cut ginger into matchstick strips. Chop garlic. Cut onion into half, then lengthwise into 2 cm wide wedges.

Heat oil in frying pan over moderately high heat. Add onion and garlic and stir-fry until onion turns translucent. Add ginger, fish, bean sauce and sugar. Stir-fry for 2–3 minutes or until fish is cooked. Add celery leaves before removing from heat. Mix well.

Place fish on a serving dish and sprinkle coriander leaves and pepper on top.

CRAB FRIED IN SALT

CUA RANG MUOI

	5 medium-sized fresh crabs
5 Tbsps	salt
3 Tbsps	oil
	6 cloves garlic, slightly crushed
2 Tbsps	vinegar
2 Tbsps	soya sauce
4 Tbsps	sugar
3 Tbsps	oyster sauce
1 cup	chicken stock
¼ Tsp	pepper

If crabs are still alive, kill them by piercing in the middle through the underbelly.

Soak crabs in water for 15–20 minutes to soften dirt around shell. Then wash thoroughly with a clean, hard brush. Make sure to remove all the mud. Drain in a colander. Remove shell and spongy part underneath it. Crack each claw with hammer or pestle. Chop crabs into four. Mix salt with enough water to cover them. Marinate crabs in salted water for 3 hours.

Remove crabs from water and steam in a steamer for 10 minutes.

Heat oil over moderate heat. Add garlic and stir-fry until golden brown. Remove garlic from oil. Add crabs and stir-fry for 10 minutes. Add vinegar, soya sauce, sugar, oyster sauce and chicken stock. Stir-fry for 10 minutes. Remove from heat. Serve with pepper sprinkled on top, and the following dip.

Chop fried garlic finely and mix with 1 tablespoon salt and 1 teaspoon pepper. Pour juice of half lemon on top of mixture.

Fish & Seafood

STEAMED CRAB AND PORK MINCE

CHA CUA HAP

	1 large crab
200 g	finely minced pork
30 g	mung bean vermicelli
	10 cloud ear fungi
	5 eggs
	1 large onion, minced
1 Tbsp	fish sauce
1 Tsp	sugar
¼ Tsp	monosodium glutamate (optional)
½ Tsp	pepper
2 Tbsps	oil
	coriander leaves

If crab is not already cooked, kill and wash as described in the recipe for Crab Fried in Salt on p. 50. Place crab in saucepan with just enough water to cover it. Boil for about 15 minutes or until cooked. Pull off crab meat.

Soak vermicelli in warm water for 10 minutes. Soak fungus in hot water for 20 minutes. Drain vermicelli and cut into 3 cm strips. Drain fungus and discard core. Slice fungus finely into strips as thin as toothpicks.

Separate two eggs and set yolks aside in a small bowl. Mix egg whites with remaining eggs.

Mix all ingredients together. Place mixture in a heatproof dish. Cook in a steamer with lid on, but open air-vent in lid to let part of steam out.

When mixture is cooked, brush top with egg yolks and place briefly under griller until yolks are cooked. Cut the meat-crab loaf into 5 cm diamond shapes. Place on serving dish and sprinkle with coriander leaves.

CRAB, ASPARAGUS AND SHARK'S FIN SOUP

CUA NAU MANG TAY VI CA

1 × 15 cm square	piece dried shark's fin
1 × 4 cm piece ginger, bruised	
600 g	chicken bones and 1 onion or 1.5 litres chicken stock
½ Tsp	salt
1 Tsp	sugar
2 Tbsps	fish sauce
¼ Tsp	monosodium glutamate (optional)
	1 tin asparagus, drained and cut into 4 cm pieces
200 g	crab meat, finely shredded
3 Tbsps	cornflour mixed with 6 Tbsps water
	2 eggs

Soak shark's fin overnight. Remove and discard any attached bone or dried meat; keep only the transparent bits. Bring 2 litres water to the boil and add shark's fin and ginger. Reduce heat and simmer for 2–3 hours or until shark's fin is tender and quite transparent. Drain in colander and wash thoroughly with cold water. Drain again in colander.

Boil chicken bones and onion in 3 litres water and ½ teaspoon salt for 10 minutes, skimming off foam. Reduce heat and simmer for 2–3 hours or until stock is reduced by half. Strain stock through strainer or a piece of cheesecloth. Reboil stock. Add seasoning: sugar, fish sauce and monosodium glutamate (if desired). Add shark's fin and asparagus and simmer for a further 30 minutes.

Add crab meat and stir gently. While soup is still simmering, add cornflour mixture to thicken, and stir well. Beat eggs for 1 minute in a bowl and then pour eggs slowly along the prongs of a fork over the whole surface of the soup.

Sprinkle with coriander leaves before serving.

Fish & Seafood

BRAISED FISH IN FISH SAUCE

CA KHO MAN

1 kg	whole fish (mullet or bream)
	5 spring onions
	1 chilli
1 L	water
¼ Tsp	salt
1 Tbsp	sugar
3 Tbsps	fish sauce
	1 small lemon

Wash and scale fish, and cut it into 4 cm pieces. Bruise 3 spring onions and the chilli with the flat part of a chopper. Cut all spring onions into 4 pieces.

Boil water in saucepan over moderate heat. Add salt, sugar, fish sauce, bruised spring onions and chilli; then add fish. Boil for 20 minutes, skimming off foam. Reduce heat and simmer for another 20 minutes.

Remove from heat. Add remaining spring onions and juice of 1 lemon before serving.

BRAISED FISH IN COCONUT JUICE

CA KHO NUOC DUA

1 kg	whole fish (mullet or bream)
4 Tbsps	fish sauce
¼ Tsp	salt
1 Tbsp	sugar (if using coconut juice)
1 Tsp	caramel sauce (see p. 89)
	juice of 1 coconut or 500 mL water with 2 tablespoons sugar
500 mL	water

Wash and scale fish, and cut it into 4 cm pieces. Marinate fish in fish sauce, salt, sugar and caramel sauce for 1 hour.

Boil juice and water in a saucepan over moderate heat. Add fish and marinade. Make sure there is enough liquid to cover fish. Boil for 5 minutes, skimming off foam. Reduce heat and simmer for 30 minutes.

Fish & Seafood

PORK AND PRAWNS FRIED WITH LEMON GRASS

TOM RIEM XA VOI THIT HEO

300 g	raw prawns
300 g	belly pork *(without skin)*
	1 medium onion
2 Tbsps	oil
	4 cloves garlic, finely chopped
1 Tbsp	chopped lemon grass
½ Tsp	salt
3 Tbsps	fish sauce
1 Tbsp	sugar
½ Tsp	caramel sauce *(see p. 89)*
⅓ cup	water

Prepare prawns as on p. 12.

Slice meat thinly (3 mm thick, 3 cm × 4 cm slices). Slice onion lengthwise into strips 1 cm wide.

Heat oil over moderate heat. Add garlic, onion and lemon grass. Stir-fry until onion turns slightly golden. Add meat and stir-fry for 2 minutes or until meat changes colour. Add prawns and stir-fry for 1 minute. Add seasonings, caramel sauce and water. Cook over low heat for 5–10 minutes until most of the water has evaporated.

DEEP-FRIED PRAWNS IN BATTER

TOM LANG BOT CHIEN

700 g	raw prawns
	fresh coconut juice *(optional)*
¼ Tsp	salt
¼ Tsp	monosodium glutamate *(optional)*
	batter for frying *(see p. 31)*
	sweet and sour sauce *(see p. 41)*
	oil for deep-frying

Prepare prawns as on p. 12, leaving on tails.

If fresh coconut juice is available, soak prawns in juice for 1 hour. Remove them from juice and squeeze them dry. Mix prawns with ¼ teaspoon salt and ¼ teaspoon monosodium glutamate (optional).

Heat oil over moderate heat. Take each prawn by the tail, dip it into the batter, making sure it is well covered with batter, and drop it into the hot oil. Deep-fry until golden brown. Remove prawns from oil and put them in a colander. (Do not put them on paper towels, as they tend to make the batter less crunchy.)

These prawns can be eaten with sweet and sour sauce or wrapped in lettuce and mint and dipped in the special garlic and lemon fish sauce (see p. 89).

Fish & Seafood

STEAMED FISH IN BEAN SAUCE

CA CHUN

1 kg	whole fish *(firm-fleshed)*
2 Tbsps	bean sauce
1 Tbsp	sugar
20 g	Chinese dried mushrooms
20 g	cloud ear fungus
20 g	golden needles or lily buds *(optional)*
50 g	mung bean vermicelli
1 × 3 cm	piece of ginger
	1 large onion
	handful coriander leaves

Wash and scale fish. Make diagonal incision into fish. Cut fish in half if no large steamer is available. Rub half of bean sauce and sugar into fish and let it stand for 1 hour.

Soak mushrooms, fungus, golden needles and vermicelli in warm water for 15 minutes. Remove from water and wash well in clean water. Remove and discard stems from mushrooms and hard core of fungus. Cut mushrooms and fungus into 2 or 4 pieces, depending on size. Remove centre part of golden needles. Cut vermicelli into 10 cm strips. Cut ginger into matchstick strips. Slice onion lengthwise thinly into 5 mm wedges.

Mix above ingredients with remaining salt, sugar and bean sauce. Place half the mixture in a large ovenproof dish and place fish on top. Sprinkle remaining mixture on top of fish, and then 1 tablespoon of water.

Steam in a steamer for half to three-quarters of an hour.

Serve sprinkled with coriander leaves.

Poultry

CHICKEN ROASTED WITH FIVE SPICE
(Ga Nuong Ngu Vi Huong) p. 68

SPECIAL STEAMED RICE
WITH FRIED CHICKEN AND VEGETABLES
(Com Tho Ga) opposite

Poultry

SPECIAL STEAMED RICE WITH FRIED CHICKEN AND VEGETABLES

COM THO GA

This dish, 'rice cooked in a bowl', is so called because, instead of being cooked in an ordinary saucepan, the rice is prepared in a special way and then steamed in an individual bowl for each person.

Steamed rice:

	6 ovenproof small bowls or pots (*about the size of a cup*)
3 cups	rice
¼ Tsp	salt
1 Tbsp	sugar
2 Tbsps	oil
	water

Chicken dish:

	4 chicken breasts
	10 Chinese dried mushrooms
200 g	**fresh mushrooms** (*preferably unopened*)
	2 celery sticks
	2 leaves of Chinese cabbage *or* **ordinary cabbage**
	2 medium carrots
	1 red capsicum (pepper)
	1 large onion
	5 cloves garlic
4 Tbsps	oil
½ Tsp	salt
1 Tbsp	sugar
2 Tbsps	oyster sauce
1 Tsp	sesame seed oil
2 Tbsps	soya sauce
2 Tbsps	cornflour
1 Tbsp	chopped coriander leaves (*optional*)
1 Tsp	spring onions (*optional*)

Prepare the rice first as it takes about one hour to cook.

Wash rice thoroughly (see p. 13) and pour it into a small mixing bowl. Mix in salt, sugar and oil. Half fill the bowls with rice. Add water to rice until it is about 1.5 cm above the rice. Place bowls in a large steamer and steam for 1 hour. Check that water in the steamer does not evaporate. Cut chicken into 4 × 1 cm slices. Soak Chinese mushrooms for 30 minutes in hot water. Remove stems. Cut mushrooms into 4. Wash vegetables and cut into 4 cm × 1 cm strips. Cut onion into half lengthwise. Then cut again lengthwise into strips 1 cm wide. Slice garlic finely.

Heat 2 tablespoons oil over moderate heat in a large frying pan. Add ¼ teaspoon salt and then half of the garlic and onion. Stir-fry until onion becomes translucent. Add 1 tablespoon sugar and then Chinese mushrooms. Stir-fry over low heat for 2 minutes, then increase heat to medium. Add carrots, cabbage, celery, capsicum and fresh mushrooms in that order. Stir-fry for 1 minute after adding each vegetable. Stir-fry until vegetables change colour but still remain crunchy. Do not overcook. Add 2 tablespoons water if necessary. Remove from frying pan.

Heat remaining oil in the frying pan over moderate heat. Add the remaining salt, onion and garlic. Stir-fry until onion becomes translucent. Add chicken. Stir-fry for 2 minutes until chicken is cooked then slightly increase heat. Add vegetables, soya sauce, oyster sauce and sesame seed oil. Mix vegetables and chicken. Mix corn-flour with ½ cup water. When the sauce in the frying pan starts boiling add cornflour and water. Mix well. Serve immediately with coriander and spring onion leaves if available. Otherwise parsley would be adequate.

Poultry

BOILED CHICKEN AND RICE

COM GA LUOT

	1 chicken (1.5 kg)
1 Tsp	salt
2 L	water
	3 stalks spring onion
3 Tbsps	oil
1 Tsp	sesame seed oil
1 kg	rice
	1 cinnamon stick, 5 cm long
	1 small onion
	5 cloves garlic, chopped finely

Dipping sauce:

1 Tbsp	minced ginger
1 Tbsp	vinegar
	pinch of salt
1½ Tbsps	soya sauce

Wash chicken. Rub inside with 1 teaspoon salt. Boil 2 litres water in large saucepan. Drop chicken in saucepan together with 2 stalks spring onion cut into 7 cm lengths. When water boils again, reduce heat to simmer. Simmer for 45 minutes. Test if chicken is cooked by pricking a fork into abdomen or thigh. If no blood oozes out then chicken is cooked. Otherwise keep simmering for another 15 minutes until chicken is cooked.

Remove chicken from pan; keep stock aside. Wash chicken thoroughly in cold water. Soak chicken in cold water and then renew water. Repeat process twice. Remove chicken from water and let dry in a cool place for 1 hour.

Mix 1 tablespoon oil with sesame seed oil and brush all over chicken. Chop it into bite-sized pieces.

Wash rice thoroughly and let drain in colander for 30 minutes.

Heat 2 tablespoons oil in a saucepan over moderate heat. Add cinnamon, chopped onion and garlic. Stir-fry until onion turns golden, and then add rice. Stir-fry until rice turns translucent. Add chicken stock to rice. Bring water to the boil. Stir frequently to stop rice from sticking to pan. Reduce heat to low. Cover with lid and let simmer for 20 minutes before serving.

Mix all sauce ingredients together.

How to serve:
Serve rice in individual bowls. Dip chicken pieces in sauce and eat with rice and fried vegetables.

CHICKEN ROASTED IN BUTTER

GA NUONG BEURRE

	1 chicken (2 kg)
1 Tsp	salt
1 Tsp	ground pepper
½ Tsp	monosodium glutamate (optional)
	4 large cloves garlic
50 g	butter (melted)
2 Tsps	sugar

Wash and dry chicken with cloth or paper towels. Hang by the neck in an airy place to dry. Crush garlic and mix with salt, pepper and monosodium glutamate. Rub ⅔ of this mixture into chicken inside and outside. Rub 1 teaspoon of butter inside the chicken. Let chicken stand for half a day in a cool place.

Mix the rest of garlic, salt and pepper mixture with sugar and butter. Preheat oven to 180°C (350°F). Place chicken on its back on a rack in a baking dish. After 20 minutes bring chicken out and brush it thoroughly with the seasoned butter. Return chicken to oven.

Repeat this process twice before chicken is cooked (about 1–1½ hours).

Poultry

CHICKEN FRIED IN TURMERIC SAUCE

GA XAO LAN

	1 chicken (1.5 kg)
200 g	desiccated coconut or 50 g coconut cream mixed with 3 cups hot water
	3 gloves garlic
	1 large onion
1½ Tbsps	turmeric
½ Tsp	salt
1 Tbsp	finely minced lemon grass
1 Tsp	ground bean sauce
	oil for frying

If using desiccated coconut, extract milk by method indicated on p. 14. Keep aside ⅓ cup of the first extract (*nuoc cot dua*). If using coconut cream, cut block into 5 mm strips and add hot water. Keep aside ⅓ cup of this mixture.

Wash and dry chicken. Chop into bite-sized pieces. Cut onion into half lengthwise and then into 1 cm wide wedges. Chop garlic finely.

Heat oil in large frying pan. Add onion and garlic and then chicken. Stir-fry until meat changes colour. Add remaining ingredients except ⅓ cup coconut milk. Cook over moderate heat for 30 minutes or until meat is cooked. Stir occasionally and add ½ cup water if necessary to keep meat from burning.

Remove from heat when chicken is cooked and sauce has thickened. Add remaining coconut milk. Sprinkle ground roasted peanuts and chopped coriander leaves on top.

A special fish and coconut sauce can accompany this dish. See p. 89.

DUCK RICE PORRIDGE

CHAO VIT

	1 small duck (1.5 kg)
⅔ cup	rice
¼ Tsp	salt
2.5 L	water
50 g	mung beans (shelled)
2 Tbsps	fish sauce
½ Tsp	monosodium glutamate (optional)
½ Tsp	pepper
1 Tbsp	chopped coriander leaves
1 Tbsp	spring onions

Sauce:

	1 piece ginger (3 cm long)
	1 clove garlic
⅓ cup	fish sauce
2 Tbsps	sugar
2 Tbsps	vinegar
2 Tbsps	boiled water

Wash and dry duck. Bring water to the boil, add salt, duck and rice. Boil for 30 minutes on medium heat and then add mung beans, previously washed. Remove duck from stock when cooked (it takes about 1½ hours). Continue boiling rice and beans until soft. Then add fish sauce and monosodium glutamate.

Chop duck into small pieces. Serve porridge with pepper, coriander leaves and spring onions.

To make the sauce, mince garlic and ginger finely. Mix garlic and ginger with remaining ingredients. Stir well to dissolve sugar.

How to eat this dish:
Serve porridge in a bowl. Dip pieces of duck in ginger fish sauce. Eat meat and then a mouthful of porridge.

Poultry

CHICKEN AND CABBAGE SALAD

GA XE PHAY

	1 small chicken *(1 kg)*
	1 large onion
½ cup	vinegar
½ Tsp	salt
1 Tbsp	sugar
½ Tsp	fish sauce
	¼ cabbage *(finely shredded)*
⅓ cup	chopped Vietnamese mint *(rau ram) or* ordinary mint

Wash chicken and boil until tender (about 1 hour). Remove chicken from the stock and let cool. Remove skin and bones, and shred the chicken meat.

Peel onion and cut in half, then slice finely. Marinate onion in vinegar, salt and sugar for 30 minutes. Mix chicken, cabbage, onion with fish sauce and half the mint leaves. Sprinkle the remaining mint on top of the salad before serving.

This chicken and cabbage salad can be served as a side salad or it can accompany rice porridge. See p. 66 for the rice porridge.

CHICKEN CURRY, INDIAN STYLE

CARI CHA

	1 chicken *(2 kg)*
300 g	desiccated coconut
1 Tbsp	coconut cream
4 Tbsps	curry paste
	5 bay leaves
1 × 5 cm	piece ginger
	2 medium onions
1½ Tsps	salt
1 Tsp	sugar
50 g	ghee *(unsalted clarified butter)*
1 Tbsp	oil
	4 large potatoes

Mince ginger and onions together. Wash and dry chicken and cut into medium-sized curry pieces. Rub salt, sugar, curry paste and half of onion mixture into chicken and let stand for 30 minutes.

Peel potatoes and cut into quarters. Let stand in water.

Heat ghee in large saucepan or casserole over moderate heat. Add the remainder of onion mixture. Fry until onion turns translucent. Fry chicken until meat changes colour. Add 5 bay leaves, 500 mL of coconut milk and some water until it is 4 cm above meat. Simmer for 1½ hours *without* lid or until stock turns into gravy.

Dry potatoes and fry in 1 tablespoon oil until golden. Add potatoes to curry after it has simmered for almost an hour. Remove curry from heat and add ⅓ cup of first extract of coconut milk.

This dish is usually eaten with rice cooked in a special way (see recipe for Indian Rice, p. 64), salads and pickles.

Poultry

CHICKEN AND MUSHROOM PAELLA

GA NAU COM TAY CAM

	1 chicken *(about 1.5 kg)*
	1 medium-sized onion
	3 cloves garlic
	1 piece ginger *(about 5 cm long)*
	salt and pepper *(a pinch)*
1 Tbsp	sugar
1 Tbsp	soya sauce
2 Tbsps	oyster sauce
200 g	straw mushrooms *or* ordinary mushrooms
3 cups	rice
	15 Chinese mushrooms
3 Tbsps	oil
¼ Tsp	salt
3 cups	water
2 Tsps	sesame seed oil

Wash chicken and dry well. Chop into small pieces (about 5 cm long and 2.5 cm wide). Mince onion, garlic and ginger together. Then add onion mixture to chicken together with salt, pepper, sugar, soya and oyster sauce. Mix well. Let stand for 30–60 minutes.

Wash fresh mushrooms and cut into quarters. Wash rice and let it drain in a colander. Soak Chinese mushrooms in hot water for 30 minutes. Remove from water and squeeze dry. Discard stems. Heat 1 tablespoon oil in a frying pan and add 1 teaspoon salt. Fry Chinese mushrooms over low heat for 2 minutes (until mushrooms have puffed up). Remove from frying pan and cut into quarters.

Heat 2 tablespoons oil in a large casserole over medium heat. Add the chicken mixture and continue stirring until chicken changes colour. Add 1 cup water, cover and cook on moderate heat for 45 minutes, stirring from time to time to prevent meat sticking. Meanwhile, mix all mushrooms with remaining onion mixture.

When chicken is cooked, remove it from the casserole. Add rice to the casserole with 2 cups water. Cover and cook over moderate heat for 30 minutes, adding water if necessary. (Make sure that rice does not become mushy.) Then simmer for another 30 minutes, stirring occasionally to avoid sticking.

Fry the mushrooms and chicken together for 5 minutes until mushrooms are cooked, then add sesame seed oil. Add chicken and mushrooms to the rice. Mix well, but gently, to make sure chicken pieces don't disintegrate. Cover and simmer for 10 minutes, stirring occasionally.

This dish can be eaten with a western-style salad or steamed vegetables.

FRIED RICE WITH TOMATO PASTE

COM RANG CA TOMATE

6 cups	boiled rice
2 Tbsps	oil
	1 medium onion *(minced)*
	4 cloves garlic *(chopped)*
3 Tbsps	tomato paste
½ Tsp	salt
½ Tsp	sugar
3 oz	butter
2 cups	cooked green peas *(frozen peas may be used but not canned peas)*

Heat oil in large frying pan over moderate heat. Add onion and garlic. Fry until onion changes colour; add tomato paste. Fry for 1 minute and add rice, salt and pepper. Mix well for 2 minutes, add butter and mix well. Add peas and mix well again for 2 minutes.

Serve immediately, to be eaten warm.

Poultry

CHICKEN DEEP-FRIED IN BATTER WITH SWEET AND SOUR SAUCE

GA LAN BOT CHIEN SAUCE CHUA NGOT

	1 chicken *(1 kg)*
	batter *(see p. 31)*
	oil for deep frying

Sauce:

	½ cucumber
	1 large onion
	4 cloves garlic
	1 small carrot
	¼ cauliflower *or* 4 celery sticks *(depending on season)*
	1 tomato peeled and chopped
	5 pickled leeks *or* small pickled onions
4 cm	ginger
½ Tsp	salt
1 Tbsp	soya sauce
1 Tbsp	white vinegar
2 Tbsps	sugar
1 Tbsp	oyster sauce
1 Tsp	sesame seed oil
2 Tbsps	cornflour mixed with 1 cup water
2 Tbsps	oil

Make batter and let it stand for 4 or 5 hours before using. Wash and dry chicken. Chop into small pieces (6 cm × 3 cm). Keep aside in fridge. Meanwhile prepare sauce.

Cut cucumber into half lengthwise. Remove and discard seeds and pith. Cut each half into halves again lengthwise. Cut carrot into 4 pieces lengthwise. Then cut carrot and cucumber diagonally into 5 mm thick pieces. Mix with 1 tablespoon salt and let stand for 30 minutes. Mix vegetables well, wash and remove excess water to make them crunchy.

Cut celery diagonally into 1 cm thick pieces; cauliflower into small pieces (2 cm × 2 cm). Cut onion into 15 mm wedges. Chop garlic and slice pickled onion or leek. Peel and cut ginger into matchstick-sized pieces.

Heat oil in frying pan over moderate heat. Add salt, onion and 3 cloves garlic. Stir-fry until onion turns translucent. Add carrots. Stir-fry for one minute then add celery or cauliflower. Stir-fry another minute and add cucumber. Stir-fry for 2 minutes. Add tomato, pickled onion or leeks and water if necessary. Remove vegetables from frying pan. Keep aside.

Heat 1 tablespoon oil. Add garlic and ginger. Stir-fry for one minute until fragrant. Then add all liquid ingredients. Stir continuously until sauce thickens. Add vegetables to sauce before serving.

Heat about 500 mL oil in deep frying pan. Dip chicken in batter and then drop it into oil; fry until golden. Drain fat off and arrange chicken pieces on serving plate. Pour sauce on top of chicken. Sprinkle with a dash of pepper or some chopped coriander leaves.

Dip in soya sauce when eating.

DEEP-FRIED CHICKEN WINGS

CANH GA CHIEN BEURRE

1 kg	chicken wings
½ Tsp	salt
1 Tsp	pepper
½ Tsp	monosodium glutamate *(optional)*
	oil for deep frying
200 g	flour
3 Tbsps	melted butter

Wash chicken wings and dry well. Mix salt, pepper and monosodium glutamate. Rub the mixture into chicken wings. Let stand for 2 hours.

Heat enough oil for deep frying. Dip wings in flour, covering well. Then cook in oil until golden brown. Remove from oil and brush with butter. Serve hot.

Poultry

CHICKEN STUFFED WITH GLUTINOUS RICE

GA DON COM NEP

	1 chicken (1.5 kg)
1 Tsp	salt
¼ Tsp	pepper
½ Tsp	sugar
	1 onion, minced
2 cups	glutinous rice
200 g	straw mushrooms *or* ordinary mushrooms
	2 slices ham
2 Tbsps	oil
	1 lemon
	oil for deep frying
3 Tbsps	butter

Wash and dry chicken and place on a large board. Using a sharp knife, cut chicken from neck to abdomen. Separate meat from bone, leaving the two wings on. Now cut meat away from skin carefully so as not to tear skin. Dice chicken meat and mix with salt, pepper, sugar and onion. Simmer chicken bones in 1.5 litres water and ½ teaspoon salt for 2 hours. Remove bones from stock.

Wash glutinous rice. Bring stock to the boil and then add rice to it, cover saucepan and boil for another 5 minutes, stirring occasionally to stop rice from sticking to pan. Reduce heat and simmer for another 20 minutes.

Wash mushrooms thoroughly and then dice (remove stems from ordinary mushrooms). Dice the ham.

Heat oil in frying pan. Fry chicken and onion with mushrooms. Stir for 5 minutes until meat is cooked. Add rice to chicken, toss well, add ham and mix well. Let the mixture cool. Sew the chicken skin together with cotton, leaving an opening at the end for the stuffing. Fill chicken with above mixture. Make sure not to press too hard so as not to tear skin. When chicken is filled, sew up the opening.

Brush juice of lemon all over chicken. Heat 500 mL oil in deep frying pan over moderate heat. Fry chicken until golden. Remove chicken from oil and brush butter all over. Serve chicken sliced.

ROAST DUCK

VIT QUAY

	1 duck (about 2 kg)
4 Tsps	char siu powder *or*
2 Tsps	five spice powder
2 Tbsps	soya sauce
2 Tbsps	sugar
½ Tsp	monosodium glutamate *(optional)*
1 Tsp	honey
½ cup	water

Wash duck thoroughly; then pour boiling water over it. Dry thoroughly. Prick duck all over with a sharp skewer. Hang duck in an airy cool place (away from insects) for 2 hours or more.

Mix *char siu* powder with soya sauce, sugar and monosodium glutamate. Rub the mixture into duck, inside and outside. Marinate for 1 hour.

Heat oven to 200°C (400°F). Wipe the duck skin until thoroughly dry. Mix honey with water and brush duck with honey mixture. Place duck breast down on a rack in a baking dish. Roast for 1½ hours until cooked. Test if duck is cooked by pricking a skewer in the leg. If blood still appears then the duck is not cooked.

A chicken could be used instead of the duck, but the cooking time would only be about 1 hour.

Poultry

SPECIAL FRIED RICE

COM BAI LAI

4 cups	rice
200 g	frozen peas
	½ chicken (500 g)
200 g	crab meat
100 g	ham
	1 large carrot
	4 large cloves garlic
	1 large onion
1 L	coconut milk (see p. 14)
500 mL	water
½ Tsp	salt
1 Tbsp	sugar
50 g	butter
	5 egg yolks
3 Tbsps	oil
2 Tsps	soya sauce
¼ Tsp	monosodium glutamate (optional)

Wash rice and let dry for 30 minutes. Boil peas, drain and keep aside. Roast chicken (see recipe for Chicken Roasted in Butter, p. 58) and then shred flesh into fine strips (as thin as toothpicks). Shred crab meat finely, cut ham into fine strips, dice carrot and chop garlic. Slice onion lengthwise into 1 cm wide strips.

Boil coconut milk and water together. Add salt and sugar and then rice; cover with lid. Boil for 5 minutes, stirring occasionally to prevent sticking. Pour out excess liquid. Reduce heat and simmer for 35 minutes. Because the rice is cooked with coconut milk, it takes longer to cook and can burn if the heat is too high. Stir occasionally to make sure it does not burn.

When rice is cooked, add butter and mix well. Add egg yolks one by one and mix well with a large wooden spoon. Keep rice on a very low heat.

Meanwhile heat oil in frying pan over moderate heat. Fry onion and garlic until golden, then add carrot, chicken, crab, peas, soya sauce and monosodium glutamate and stir-fry for 2 minutes.

Dish rice in a large bowl. Arrange chicken mixture and ham on top. Garnish with a few sprigs of coriander and a dash of ground pepper.

INDIAN RICE

COM NI

4 cups	rice
8 cups	coconut milk (see p. 14)
50 g	sultanas
50 g	roasted unsalted cashew nuts
	5 bay leaves
	10 cloves
	2 anise stars
1 × 5 cm	piece cinnamon stick
	1 small onion
1 × 2 cm	piece ginger
1 Tsp	sugar
¼ Tsp	salt
50 g	ghee

Wash and drain rice; let dry for 1 hour.

Mince onion and ginger. Wrap cloves, anise and cinnamon in a piece of cheesecloth and tie into a bag.

Heat ghee in a large saucepan over moderate heat. Add onion and ginger, fry until onion turns translucent and add coconut milk, salt, sugar, spice and bay leaves. When milk starts boiling, add rice. Boil for 5 minutes over moderate heat, stirring occasionally to stop rice from sticking. When milk has been absorbed, add sultanas and cashew nuts. Reduce heat. Mix well, cover with a tight-fitting lid and simmer for 20–30 minutes. Stir occasionally.

Poultry

STUFFED DUCK SOUP AND VERMICELLI

VIT TIEM

	1 duck *(1.5 kg)*
¼ Tsp	salt
50 g	dry lotus seeds
50 g	raw unsalted peanuts
50 g	ginkgo nuts *(optional)*
50 g	water chestnuts *or* carrots
50 g	Chinese dried plums
	10 dried Chinese mushrooms
50 g	small onions *(about the size of pickling onions)*
2 Tbsps	fish sauce
	juice of 1 coconut *or* 1 Tbsp sugar mixed with 1L water
2L	water

Garnish:

250 g	rice vermicelli
200 g	bean sprouts
	5 lettuce leaves
	handful of mint
	hoisin sauce for dipping

Wash duck well, remove any pads of fat and then dry. Rub salt into duck. Leave aside.

Soak lotus seeds, peanuts and ginkgo nuts overnight. Remove skins. Also remove the green stem from the centre of the lotus seeds and ginkgo nuts. Cook lotus seeds and peanuts in water over moderate heat for 30 minutes until tender; remove from heat and wash in cold water.

Peel water chestnuts and cut into quarters. Remove stones from plums and cut into halves. Soak Chinese mushrooms for 30 minutes in hot water. Remove from water and discard stems. Cut mushrooms into quarters.

Mix all ingredients together and stuff duck with mixture. When duck is filled, sew up openings.

Place duck in a large saucepan and cover it with coconut juice and water. Bring soup to the boil and then simmer on low heat for 1½ hours until duck is tender. Skim occasionally. Do not overcook duck. Check seasonings before serving.

Boil vermicelli in water for 5 to 10 minutes until soft, wash in cold water and drain well. Blanch bean sprouts for 2 minutes and let cool. Slice lettuce and mint finely. Mix vegetables together.

To serve:

In each preheated individual bowl, put ⅓ bowl vermicelli, 2 tablespoons bean sprout salad, some of the duck pieces and 1 tablespoon of the filling. Dip duck pieces in hoisin sauce to lift the flavour of the soup.

Poultry

CHICKEN COOKED IN COCONUT AND CURRY SAUCE WITH VERMICELLI

GA NAU CARI NUOC DUA

	1 chicken (2 kg)
300 g	desiccated coconut
1 Tbsp	coconut cream (optional)
3 Tbsps	curry powder
	2 sweet potatoes (about 20 cm long) or 4 potatoes
	2 stalks lemon grass or 2 Tbsps dried chopped lemon grass (wrapped in a piece of cheesecloth).
	1 large onion
	3 cloves garlic
1 Tsp	sugar
1½ Tsps	salt
3 Tbsps	oil

Garnish:

250 g	medium rice vermicelli
	bean sprout salad (see p. 65)
1 Tbsp	salt
	1 chilli (optional)
	1 lemon

Extract milk from desiccated coconut as indicated on p. 14. Reserve ⅓ cup of first extract (nuoc cot dua).

Wash and dry chicken and cut into bite-sized pieces. Peel and cut potatoes likewise and let stand in water to stop browning. Crush garlic with the flat part of a knife. Cut onion lengthwise into segments.

Heat oil in large saucepan over moderate heat and fry onion and garlic until onion turns translucent. Add chicken, stir-fry until chicken changes colour (turns white). Add salt and sugar; stir-fry. Then add curry powder, mix well and pour in coconut milk until it is 5 cm above meat.

Cook over low heat for 1½ hours or until chicken is tender.

Fry potatoes in 1 tablespoon oil until slightly gold. Add potatoes to chicken 30 minutes before finishing time.

When meat is cooked, remove pot from heat and add first extract of coconut milk and cream.

Boil vermicelli for 10 minutes. Wash and drain. Cut lemon into quarters to be served at the table. Grind chilli and mix with salt. In each individual bowl place ⅓ bowl vermicelli and 2 tablespoons bean sprout salad. Pour chicken curry soup over the contents.

Serve with lemon and salt, if required.

CHICKEN RICE PORRIDGE

CHAO GA

	1 small chicken
⅔ cup	rice
2.5 L	water
½ Tsp	monosodium glutamate (optional)
1 Tbsp	fish sauce
1 Tbsp	chopped spring onions
1 Tbsp	chopped coriander leaves
½ Tsp	pepper

Fry rice until it turns opaque (do not let brown).

Bring water to the boil. Add chicken and rice.

Remove chicken from stock when cooked (about 45 minutes). Use chicken to make salad as shown in preceding recipe. Continue cooking rice until soft. Then add fish sauce and monosodium glutamate.

Serve porridge with pepper, coriander leaves and spring onions, and chicken and cabbage salad.

How to eat this dish:
Pour soup into a bowl. Put chicken salad on a side dish.

Eat soup and salad alternately. Dip salad in lemon and garlic fish sauce (see p. 89) before eating. Do not mix the salad in the soup. It would lose its own flavour.

Poultry

CHICKEN IN LEMON GRASS AND CHILLI

GA XAO XA OT

	1 chicken *(about 1.5 kg)*
	4 cloves garlic
	1 large onion
3 Tbsps	oil
50 g	lemon grass *(finely minced)*
1 Tsp	ground dried chillies *or* 1 fresh chilli, about 4 cm long, minced *(optional)*
4 Tbsps	fish sauce
1 Tbsp	sugar
1 Tbsp	caramel sauce *(see p. 89)*
1 cup	water

Wash chicken and dry well. Cut chicken into small pieces. Peel garlic and slice it finely. Cut onion into halves lengthwise and then cut lengthwise into pieces 1 cm wide.

Heat oil in a large frying pan over medium heat. Add a pinch of salt and then garlic and onion. Fry onion and garlic until onion becomes translucent. Add lemon grass and chilli. Fry for 1–2 minutes until fragrant. Add chicken. Stir well until chicken changes colour, then add fish sauce, sugar and caramel sauce. Mix well.

Add 1 cup of water and cook over moderate heat for 45 minutes or until cooked. Stir occasionally and check that the liquid has not completely evaporated. Add more water if necessary.

CHICKEN AND RICE VERMICELLI SOUP

BUN THANG

	1 medium chicken *(1 kg)*
½ Tsp	salt
	1 large onion
3 Tbsps	fish sauce
	4 eggs
200 g	ham meat loaf

Garnish:

500 g	medium rice vermicelli
300 g	bean sprouts
	3 lettuce leaves
	handful Vietnamese mint
	shrimp sauce

Boil 3 litres water in large saucepan, add salt, onion and chicken, and boil for 5 minutes. Skim, reduce heat and simmer for 1 hour then remove chicken from stock. Add fish sauce to stock. Check the seasoning.

Beat eggs with 1 teaspoon fish sauce for 1 minute. Divide egg mixture into 4 parts and fry separately in pan to make thin omelettes. Cut omelettes into fine strips (as thin as toothpicks). Cut meat loaf or ham likewise. Shred chicken into fine strips.

Boil vermicelli in 2 litres water until soft, drain in a colander and rinse with cold water. Blanch bean sprouts for 1 minute and let cool. Cut lettuce and mint into fine strips. Mix bean sprouts, lettuce and mint.

How to serve:
Before serving, bring stock to boiling point.

In each preheated individual bowl, place a handful of vermicelli, 2 tablespoons bean sprout salad, 1 tablespoon chicken, ½ tablespoon ham and ½ tablespoon omelette. Then pour hot chicken stock on top. Add ⅛ teaspoon shrimp sauce and a dash of chilli sauce, if desired.

Poultry

FRIED WHOLE CHICKEN

GA ROTI

Although the name of this dish borrows from the French word *rôti* meaning 'roasted', the method of cooking does not involve any roasting at all.

	1 chicken *(1.5 kg)*
	6 large cloves garlic
1 Tsp	salt
1 Tsp	pepper
¼ Tsp	monosodium glutamate *(optional)*
3 Tbsps	oil
1 Tbsp	sugar
2 Tbsps	butter

Wash and dry chicken and cut into four pieces. Peel garlic and slice finely. Make several slits in chicken. Insert garlic into slits. Mix salt, pepper and monosodium glutamate. Rub into chicken, inside and outside.

Heat 3 tablespoons of oil in large frying pan. Add chicken pieces. Fry for 2 minutes, turn over and fry for another 2 minutes. Continue turning until chicken changes colour. Cover and cook over low heat for 45 minutes or until tender.

Remove lid and add 1 teaspoon sugar and 2 tablespoons water. Cook over moderate heat. Continue turning until chicken is golden, then add butter and spread evenly over chicken. Let it stand in butter for 10 minutes. Remove from heat and cut chicken into small pieces.

This dish is usually accompanied by Fried Rice With Tomato Paste, p. 61.

CHICKEN ROASTED WITH FIVE SPICE

GA NUONG VOI NGU VI HUONG

	1 chicken *(2 kg)*
30 g	garlic
30 g	onion
4 Tsps	spiced sherry *(see p. 89)*
½ Tsp	salt
½ Tsp	ground cloves
1 Tsp	sugar
5 Tbsps	thin soya sauce
2 Tsps	thick soya sauce
½ Tsp	pepper
1 Tbsp	oil
1 Tsp	sesame seed oil

Wash and dry chicken. Mince onion and garlic with 2 teaspoons spiced sherry, ½ teaspoon salt, ½ teaspoon cloves, 1 teaspoon sugar, 1 tablespoon thin soya sauce, 1 teaspoon thick soya sauce and ½ teaspoon pepper. Rub this mixture inside chicken.

Place chicken in a bowl. Pour over the remaining soya sauces and sherry. Marinate chicken in sauce for 2 hours. Baste chicken with the marinade every 20 minutes.

Heat oven to 200°C (400°F). Place chicken on a grid in a roasting pan in the oven for 10 minutes. Brush marinade on chicken. Reduce oven temperature to moderately hot (180°C/350°F) and continue cooking, brushing chicken with marinade every 15 minutes for another 40 minutes.

After 50 minutes of cooking, brush chicken with oil and sesame oil. Continue cooking for another 20 minutes or until chicken is tender. Test if chicken is cooked by pricking a fine skewer into thigh joint of chicken. If there is blood then the chicken is not yet cooked.

Serve chicken with a lemon sauce (see p. 89) and green salad.

Beef

Beef

BEEF AND VERMICELLI A LA HUE (TO SERVE 6)

BUN BO HUE

	1 leg of pork
500 g	chuck steak
	3 bay leaves
	3 cloves
	3 cloves garlic
	1 large onion
½ Tsp	shrimp sauce
¼ Tsp	cayenne pepper
½ Tsp	monosodium glutamate (optional)
1 Tbsp	sugar
2 Tbsps	fish sauce
	2 beef stock cubes
1 Tbsp	tomato paste
	2 stalks lemon grass or 2 Tbsps chopped dried lemon grass
2 × 4 cm	pieces cinnamon
	rind of 1 lemon
1 Tsp	curry powder
1 × 6 cm	piece of ginger
⅓ Tsp	sesame oil

Wash leg of pork. Remove excess fat and half of skin.

Boil about 3 litres water in a large saucepan. Add leg of pork with lemon grass and boil for 30 minutes, skimming off foam occasionally. Add chuck steak and beef cubes. Boil for 10 minutes, skimming off foam, then reduce heat and simmer for 30 minutes. Add all other ingredients except the shrimp sauce and sesame oil. Simmer until meat is tender. Remove meat from stock and slice into bite-sized pieces. Add sesame oil to soup before serving.

This soup is eaten with vermicelli and bean sprout salad.

See p. 67 for the method of serving. Add a dash of shrimp sauce to each bowl before serving.

SKEWERED BEEF

BO LUI

1 kg	fillet steak or rump steak
	1 large onion
	4 cloves garlic
3 Tbsps	chopped lemon grass
1 Tsp	sugar
½ Tsp	salt
¼ Tsp	monosodium glutamate (optional)
2 Tbsps	oil or lard
50 g	unsalted roasted peanuts, crushed

Discard all the gristle and fat from meat. Slice meat very thinly (about 2–3 mm thick and 3 cm × 6 cm). Mince onion and garlic. Mix meat with onion, garlic, lemon grass, salt, sugar, oil, monosodium glutamate and two tablespoons crushed peanuts. Let the mixture stand for 1–2 hours.

Thread meat slices on skewers, folding each slice into two or three before threading. Do not put meat slices too close to each other or they will not cook very well.

Grill meat under griller or over charcoal fire. Sprinkle the remaining crushed peanuts on the meat before serving.

Traditionally, Vietnamese pour some spring onion fat on top of meat before eating. However, if you do not like too much fat, this can be omitted. Spring onion fat can be made by frying 2 tablespoons of chopped spring onions in ½ cup of oil and ⅓ teaspoon salt for one minute.

This dish can be eaten with boiled rice or rice vermicelli, bean sprout salad (see p. 67), cucumber and lemon and garlic fish sauce (see p. 89). Or it can be eaten with a special type of rice vermicelli (see p. 73), salad and fish sauce.

Beef

BEEF STEWED IN LEMON GRASS AND ANISEED

BO KHO

500 g	chuck steak *or* gravy beef
1.5 L	water
	2 stalks lemon grass, bruised and cut into 4 cm lengths *or* 2 Tbsps dried chopped lemon grass wrapped in cheesecloth
	3 anise stars
1 Tsp	salt
2 Tsps	sugar
	2 carrots
1 × 5 cm	piece ginger
2 Tbsps	oil
	1 medium onion, chopped
	1 clove garlic, chopped
	2 ripe tomatoes, chopped
	1 lemon
2 Tbsps	bean sauce
½ Tbsp	tomato paste
250 g	rice noodles and
200 g	bean sprout salad *(see p. 67)*

Cut meat into bite-sized pieces (3 cm cubes). Boil water in large saucepan. Add lemon grass, anise stars, 1 teaspoon salt, 2 teaspoons sugar and finally meat. Skim off foam. Let meat boil for 30 minutes over moderate heat.

Wash and peel carrots. Cut into 3 cm long pieces. Peel ginger and cut into matchstick pieces.

Remove saucepan from heat and remove meat from stock. Heat oil in frying pan over medium heat. Fry onion and garlic until onion turns translucent. Add tomatoes and ginger and stir-fry for 1 minute. Then add bean sauce and tomato paste and stir-fry for 1 minute. Add meat and stir-fry for 3 or 4 minutes. Pour contents of frying pan into stock. Replace saucepan over moderate heat. After stock starts boiling again, reduce heat and simmer for 30 minutes. Then add carrots and boil for another 20 minutes before serving.

This dish can be served as a soup with rice noodles, bean sprouts, mint and lemon. If using rice noodles, place them in boiling water and boil for 5 to 10 minutes until soft. Wash in cold water and drain well.

It can also be served as a stew with lemon and French bread.

FRIED BEEF WITH WATERCRESS SALAD

BO LUC LAC

500 g	fillet steak
	5 cloves garlic, crushed
	salt
½ Tsp	pepper
1½ Tsps	sugar
3 Tbsps	oil
	1 large onion
2 Tbsps	vinegar
2 Tbsps	salad oil
500 g	watercress *or* lettuce

Cut meat into 2 cm cubes. Mix meat with 2 cloves garlic, ½ teaspoon salt, ¼ teaspoon pepper, ½ teaspoon sugar and 1 tablespoon oil. Let meat stand in this marinade for 1 hour.

Cut onion lengthwise into 1 mm thin strips. Marinate onion in vinegar, ¼ teaspoon salt, 1 teaspoon sugar, ¼ teaspoon pepper and 2 tablespoons salad oil.

Wash watercress. Drain well and arrange on a large serving plate.

Heat 2 tablespoons oil over high heat. Add a pinch of sugar and garlic. Fry until fragrant. Add meat and stir-fry for 2 minutes, until just cooked. Put meat on top of watercress. Add a dash of soft butter, and pour onion mixture on top of meat.

FRIED BEEF WITH WATERCRESS SALAD
(Bo Luc Lac) opposite

MEAT AND SEAFOOD FONDUE
(Ta Pinh Lu Kieu Viet Nam) recipe p. 79

Beef

BEEF BALL SOUP

BO VO VIEN

500 g	chuck steak
½ Tsp	pepper
¼ Tsp	monosodium glutamate *(optional)*
1 Tsp	salt
1 Tbsp	cornflour
1 Tbsp	oil
1 Tsp	baking powder
⅓ cup	chopped spring onion
	handful coriander *(optional)*

Slice meat thinly. Mix with other ingredients. Let meat stand for 1 hour. Put it in a plastic bag and place in freezer. Leave bag in freezer for about 45 minutes, turning bag over every 10 minutes to stop the meat from freezing. Remove meat from freezer and mince very finely, a small quantity at a time. (Make sure you do not overheat mince.) If you do not have a mincer you can pound meat in a mortar.

Boil 500 mL water in a saucepan, then reduce heat so that water is simmering. Mix 1 cup of cold water with 1 teaspoon salt. Oil the palm of your left hand and put some meat into it. Close your hand, squeezing until the meat appears at the top, about the size of a walnut.

Dip a soup spoon into the salty water then scoop meat from top of left hand and drop it in the simmering water (dipping the spoon in the salted water stops the meat from sticking to the spoon). Repeat this process until meat is finished.

Remove beef balls from water when they rise to the surface or turn white.

After all the meat balls have been removed from the simmering water, add 1 litre of water, 1 teaspoon salt and ½ teaspoon monosodium glutamate. Increase heat and bring water to boil. Skim off foam. Reduce heat to low. Add beef balls to stock and simmer for 3–5 minutes.

How to serve:
Put 5 or 6 beef balls together with stock in each bowl. Sprinkle some chopped spring onions and coriander leaves on top. Add one or two drops of sesame oil. Dip beef balls in sauces: hoisin sauce, black bean sauce and lemon grass and chilli sauce.

FINE RICE VERMICELLI

BANH HOI

300 g	packet fine threads rice vermicelli
1 cup	potato flour

Soak rice vermicelli in cold water for 2 hours. Place in a colander and strain well. Place a 1–2 cm layer of vermicelli on a greased perforated steamer plate. Sprinkle flour on top. Put plate in a steamer and steam for 10 minutes or until vermicelli is soft. Repeat this process until vermicelli is finished.

Sprinkle spring onion fat (see recipe for Skewered Beef, p. 71) on top of *banh hoi* before serving.

Beef

BEEF AND RICE NOODLE SOUP

PHO BO

Those of you who have lived in Vietnam will not have forgotten the taste and aroma of Beef and Rice Noodle Soup.

This is an all-courses-in-one dish, very nutritious and aromatic. It originates from the North but has been integrated in the South as long as I can remember. It is a dish favoured by all Vietnamese, from young to old. It is usually a breakfast dish, but it is also eaten at other times of the day.

When I first came to Australia I tried to cook this soup. It tasted all right but the aroma was not quite the same. It was not until my mother gave me the full list of ingredients that I could get the aroma right.

Different *pho* stalls in Vietnam have different aromas and tastes. The cooks have their own secrets. This is one of them, and I am glad to share it with you—*bon appétit!*

1 kg	beef backbone
500 g	beef shinbone
250 g	gravy beef
3 × 6 cm	pieces of ginger
½ cup	sherry
1 Tsp	salt
	2 large onions
	5 cardamom pods
	4 anise stars
1 × 4 cm	piece of cinnamon
	4 cloves
	2 white Chinese turnips *or* ordinary ones
	3 carrots
2 Tbsps	fish sauce
½ Tsp	monosodium glutamate *(optional)*

Garnish:

500 g	fillet steak
400 g	rice noodles
300 g	bean sprouts
	1 large onion, finely sliced
1 cup	chopped spring onions
½ cup	chopped coriander leaves
	a handful of mint leaves
3 Tbsps	fish sauce
⅓ cup	hoisin sauce
	pepper
	3 sliced chillies *(optional)*
	1 lemon, cut into 6 wedges

Mince one piece of ginger and mix it with the sherry. Wash the bones and gravy beef in the sherry, then rinse with warm water. Do not wash with cold water. There is no need to wash the fillet steak.

Boil 6 litres of water in a large saucepan. Add salt, bones and gravy beef. Grill onion and ginger over high heat until the outside layer is slightly burnt. Add them to the stock. Wrap the cardamom pods, anise stars, cinnamon, and cloves in a piece of cheesecloth and tie the opening. Drop this spice bag into the soup. Then add carrots and turnips (whole). Boil over moderately high heat for 20 minutes, skimming continuously. Reduce heat and simmer for 4 hours. Skim regularly so that the stock is clear and contains less fat.

Before serving, add the fish sauce and monosodium glutamate to taste and check seasoning. Remove gravy beef from stock, slice it thinly and put it on a plate to be served at the table.

Slice fillet steak very finely (about 2 mm thick). Boil rice noodles in water for 10 minutes or until soft. Do not overcook. Wash in cold water and drain well.

To serve, place noodles in each individual bowl and put some bean sprouts on top. Place some fillet steak and onion slices in a ladle and, while the stock

Beef

is boiling, dip in the ladle and cook the meat. Pour the meat and stock on top of noodles and bean sprouts, adding enough stock to make into a soup. Sprinkle some spring onions, coriander leaves and mint on top. A few drops of fish sauce or hoisin sauce will give a lift to the flavour. Also add a few slices of gravy beef if required. Before serving, squeeze some lemon on top of soup.

SWEET AND SOUR BEEF

BO XAO GIAM

600 g	rump steak
	1 large cucumber
	1 carrot
	2 celery stalks
	2 medium tomatoes
	1 large onion
	4 cloves garlic
	salt
2 Tbsps	sugar
2 Tbsps	vinegar
1½ Tbsps	soya sauce
1 Tbsp	cornflour mixed with ⅔ cup water
3 Tbsps	oil
	handful coriander leaves (optional)

Discard fat and gristle from steak. Slice beef very thinly (2 mm thick, 5 cm × 3 cm slices). Cut off both ends of cucumber and cut it in half lengthwise. Use a spoon to remove pith and seeds. Cut cucumber in half lengthwise once again. Now slice it diagonally very thinly (2 mm thick slices). Mix cucumber with ½ tablespoon salt and let stand for 1 hour. Wash in cold water and then squeeze all the juice out.

Peel carrot and cut into four pieces lengthwise. Slice it in the same way as for the cucumber.

Separate celery leaves from stalks and cut stalks diagonally into 1 cm wide pieces. Cut celery leaves in half. Cut tomatoes lengthwise into 8 wedges (about 1 cm wide). Slice onion lengthwise into 1 cm wide wedges. Crush garlic.

Mix ¼ teaspoon salt with sugar, vinegar, soya sauce, cornflour and water in a jar.

Heat 1½ tablespoons oil over moderate heat. Add ¼ teaspoon salt, half of garlic and onion. Stir-fry until onion turns translucent. Add carrot and stir-fry for 1 minute. Then add celery and tomatoes and stir-fry for 1 minute. Add cucumber and stir-fry for 2 minutes. Add soya sauce, sugar, vinegar and cornflour. Lower heat and stir-fry until sauce thickens. Remove frying pan from heat.

In another frying pan, heat remaining oil. Add ¼ teaspoon salt and remaining onion and garlic. Stir-fry until onion turns translucent. Add meat and stir-fry for 2 minutes over high heat until meat is just cooked (do not overcook). Add vegetable sauce to meat. Stir-fry for another 2 minutes until the sauce is heated through. Serve with a dash of pepper and some chopped coriander leaves.

Beef

FRIED BEEFSTEAK WITH PEANUTS

BO XAO DAU PHONG

1 kg	fillet steak *or* rump steak
	1 large onion
	5 cloves garlic
½ Tsp	salt
1 Tsp	sugar
3 Tbsps	chopped lemon grass
¼ Tsp	monosodium glutamate *(optional)*
4 Tbsps	oil
50 g	unsalted roasted peanuts *(crushed)*

Mince ⅓ of the onion with 3 cloves garlic. Slice meat very thinly (2 mm thick, 5 cm × 3 cm slices). Mix meat with minced onion and garlic, salt, sugar, lemon grass, monosodium glutamate and 1 tablespoon oil.

Slice the rest of the onion lengthwise into segments. Crush the remaining garlic. Heat 3 tablespoons oil in frying pan over moderately high heat. Add onion and garlic and stir-fry until fragrant. Add meat and stir-fry continuously over high heat for 2 minutes or until cooked.

Sprinkle with peanuts before serving.

This dish can be eaten with boiled rice or vermicelli, bean sprout salad and lemon and garlic fish sauce (see p. 89).

Soups & Noodles

Soups & Noodles

MEAT AND SEAFOOD FONDUE

TA PINH LU KIEU VIET NAM

300 g	fillet steak
200 g	peeled raw prawns
200 g	squid
200 g	fish fillet *(bream)*
150 g	medium rice vermicelli
	20 rice papers *(see p. 10)*
	½ lettuce
	bunch mint
	½ bunch spring onions *(optional)*
	bean sauce for dipping *(see p. 39)*

Broth:

1 kg	pork bones
3 L	water
½ Tsp	salt
1 cup	white vinegar
½ cup	sugar
	1 onion, sliced

Make the broth in the morning or the night before. Boil bones in 3 litres water and ½ teaspoon salt for 20 minutes over moderate heat, skimming off the foam. Then reduce heat and simmer for about 4 hours or until the liquid is reduced by half.

Remove veins from prawns. Rub in 1 teaspoon salt. Wash until water is clear of foam.

Prepare squid as shown on p. 12. Make a dozen criss-cross cuts on the inside of squid about 5 mm apart. Cut squid into 7 cm × 3 cm strips.

Cut the fish fillets very thinly into 7 cm × 3 cm × 2 mm slices. Slice the fillet steak very thinly.

Arrange meat, fish, prawns and squid on a large plate to be placed on the table.

Wash vegetables and mint. Arrange them on a serving plate.

Before serving, mix broth, vinegar, sugar and onion together in a saucepan. Bring the mixture to the boil and pour some of it into the fondue saucepan.

How to serve:

Place meat, seafood and vegetables on the table. Place saucepan to simmer on hotplate at the table. Pour bean sauce into small individual bowls for dipping.

Using chopsticks, select some pieces of meat, seafood and vegetables and swish them around in the simmering stock. Make sure to cook the prawns and squid first because they take longer to cook. Do not overcook meat and vegetables.

Place cooked meat, seafood and vegetables on top of a piece of rice paper. Roll it up and dip roll in bean sauce. A dash of chilli sauce will give a lift to the flavour.

If using vermicelli, place cooked meat, seafood and vegetables with two tablespoons vermicelli in individual bowls. Pour bean sauce over mixture.

Soups & Noodles

PANCAKES WITH BEAN SPROUTS, PORK AND PRAWNS

BANH XEO

450 g	rice flour
1 Tbsp	sugar
½ Tsp	salt
2 Tsps	baking powder
2 cups	first extract of coconut milk *(see p. 14)*
2 Tsps	turmeric
300 g	peeled raw prawns
500 g	leg pork *or* pork fillet
750 g	bean sprouts
1 bunch	he *(optional)*
2–3 cups	second extract of coconut milk
⅓ cup	chopped spring onions
	2 large onions, sliced thinly
½ cup	shelled mung beans *(optional)*

If you want to serve this dish for dinner, start preparing the pancake mixture in the morning. Place flour in a large bowl. Add sugar, salt and baking powder. Pour in first extract of coconut milk. Knead well. Add turmeric. Knead again until turmeric is mixed through. Leave aside to rise.

Prepare prawns as described on page 12. Slice meat thinly. Wash bean sprouts and let dry in a colander. Wash *he* and cut into 5 cm sections. Mix with bean sprouts.

An hour before cooking, gradually add second extract of coconut, stirring well. Keep adding coconut milk until the mixture has the consistency of pancake mixture. Let stand for 1 hour. Add spring onions. Add more coconut milk if necessary.

Wash mung beans. Place them in a saucepan and add water until it is 2 cm over the beans. Bring to the boil, reduce heat and simmer for another 10–15 minutes until cooked. Remove excess water.

To prepare the pancakes, heat a non-stick frying pan over medium heat. Add ½ tablespoon oil.

Spread well. Add a handful of sliced onions. Stir-fry until onions turn translucent. Add half a handful of meat. Stir-fry for 1 minute. Add about 4 prawns. Stir-fry for another 2–3 minutes. Pour one ladleful of pancake mixture. Add bean sprouts, mung beans and *he*. Cover frying pan with lid for 1–2 minutes or until pancake is cooked. Before removing pancake from frying pan, fold it in half.

To speed up the cooking process, you could fry all the onions, meat and prawns at once before using with the pancakes.

To serve and eat the pancakes, each person receives a pancake which is dipped in lemon and garlic fish sauce (see p. 89) before eating. The pancake should also be accompanied with lettuce, sliced cucumber and mint.

RICE NOODLES FRIED WITH PORK AND PRAWNS

HU TIEU XAO TOM THIT

300 g	dried rice noodles
200 g	pork chop meat *or* belly pork
	1 onion
	3 cloves garlic
200 g	bean sprouts
	1 dozen *he* stems *(see p. 9)*
	5 spring onions
5 Tbsps	oil
200 g	shelled raw prawns
2 Tbsps	fish sauce

Drop noodles in 3 litres boiling water. Boil for 5–10 minutes or until noodles are tender. Drain well. Add 1 tablespoon oil to prevent stickiness.

Slice pork thinly (about 2 mm thick). Cut onion in half. Cut each half into 8 sections lengthwise. Slice garlic. Wash bean sprouts, *he*, and spring onions. Cut *he* and spring onions into 3 cm long pieces. Prepare prawns as on p. 12.

Soups & Noodles

Heat 2 tablespoons oil over moderately high heat. Add half the onion, and fry until fragrant. Add bean sprouts and *he*, and stir-fry for 1 minute. Remove and put aside.

Heat 2 tablespoons oil in same frying pan, add onion, garlic and the white parts of the spring onions. Stir-fry until onion turns translucent. Add pork and stir-fry for 2 minutes. Add prawns and stir-fry for 5 minutes. Add fish sauce, then all vegetables and noodles. Stir-fry for 2 minutes.

Serve with pepper and coriander leaves sprinkled on top.

Lemon and garlic fish sauce (see p. 89) can be added at the table.

RICE AND TAPIOCA FLOUR NOODLE SOUP WITH PORK AND PRAWNS

BANH CANH BOT LOC

Noodles:

300 g	good quality rice flour
100 g	tapioca flour *or* cornflour

Soup:

150 g	raw prawns
200 g	minced pork
	1 small onion, minced
½ Tsp	salt
1 Tsp	sugar
¼ Tsp	monosodium glutamate *(optional)*
1 Tbsp	fish sauce
	pepper
2 Tbsps	chopped spring onions
2 Tbsps	coriander leaves

In an enamel or plastic container (do not use steel or aluminium containers) with lid, mix the two types of flour with hot water. Knead vigorously and quickly so that the mixture will be doughy.

Press the dough hard into container. Pour boiling water on top until it is 4 cm above the dough. Cover tightly with lid. When the water has cooled down, pour excess water off. Mix flour with a thin wooden spoon until smooth. The consistency of the batter should be that of custard. If it is too thick, add hot water and stir well.

Bring to the boil 4 litres water in a large saucepan over moderate heat. Block the narrow ending of a funnel with your middle finger. Pour batter into it until it is two-thirds full. Place funnel over gently boiling water. Pull your finger away from the funnel opening, move the hand in a circular motion to stop the noodle streams from sticking to each other. Knock the funnel with a wooden spoon to make the batter come out.

When the noodles come to the top, scoop them out with a perforated spoon and place them in a large bowl of cold water for 2–3 minutes. Then remove from water and place in a colander to drain.

Make sure that water is not boiling too hard, otherwise the noodles will break. Add more cold water to reduce below boiling point, or reduce the heat.

Repeat the process until all the batter is cooked.

For the soup, prepare prawns as shown on p. 12. Smash them on a board with the flat part of a chopper.

Mix pork, prawns, minced onion and seasonings, and roll mixture into balls (about the size of a large cherry). Drop them into 2 litres boiling water and boil gently for 5 minutes. Skim off foam. Add 1 tablespoon fish sauce. Add noodles and boil for another 5 minutes.

Sprinkle with pepper, spring onions and coriander leaves before serving.

Soups & Noodles

CHINESE NOODLE SOUP

MI NAU TO

300 g	dried noodles *or* 500 g fresh noodles
600 g	pork bones
80 g	dried shrimps*
	1 dried squid*
	1 large onion
400 g	Xa Xiu *(roast pork)*, sliced *(see p. 32)*
	10 lettuce leaves
	10 spring onions
½ Tsp	salt
1 Tsp	sugar
2 Tbsps	fish sauce
¼ Tsp	monosodium glutamate *(optional)*
	sesame oil

Grill onion until the outside is slightly burnt. Grill squid.

Boil 4 litres water in large saucepan. Add bones, shrimps, squid and onion. Boil for 10 minutes. Skim off foam. Reduce heat and simmer for 4–5 hours. Remove squid, prawns and bones from stock. Add seasonings.

Boil noodles until soft. Drain and add 1 tablespoon oil to prevent stickiness. Separate the white part from the green part of spring onions. Chop green stems into 3 mm pieces. Blanch the white parts in boiling water for 30 seconds.

How to serve:
Place a handful of noodles in each individual soup bowl (about one-third of bowl). Cover with lettuce and 1 spring onion. Sprinkle with a few drops of sesame oil. Add boiling soup. Add 4–5 slices of roast pork.

Serve with soya sauce, vinegar (if desired), pepper and sliced chilli.

* These two items can be omitted. However, they give a special flavour quite distinct from that of ordinary soup.

CRISP FRIED NOODLES

MI XAO GION

300 g	dried thin noodles
200 g	lean pork
200 g	raw prawns
100 g	crab meat
1 × 3 cm	piece ginger
	1 large onion
	3 cloves garlic
	1 carrot
	2 celery stalks
100 g	cauliflower
100 g	cabbage, shredded
4 Tbsps	oil
¼ Tsp	salt
1 Tbsp	sugar
¼ Tsp	monosodium glutamate *(optional)*
2 Tbsps	soya sauce
1 Tbsp	oyster sauce
1 Tsp	sesame oil
2 Tbsps	cornflour, mixed with 5 Tbsps water

Prepare meat, prawns and vegetables as in recipe for Combination Fried Noodles on p. 86.

Boil noodles for 5 minutes (do not overcook). Drain well. Add 1 tablespoon oil to prevent stickiness.

Heat enough oil for deep frying in frying pan over high heat. Add noodles, a handful at a time. Stir around until crisp and golden brown. Fry vegetables, meat and prawns as in recipe for Combination Fried Noodles on p. 86.

Just before serving, add cornflour and stir well until sauce is thick. Pour meat and vegetable mixture over crisp noodles.

Soups & Noodles

RICE AND PEA STARCH NOODLE SOUP

HU TIEU NAM VANG

1 kg	pork bones
	1 large onion
4 L	water
1 Tsp	salt
2 Tbsps	fish sauce
½ Tsp	monosodium glutamate *(optional)*
200 g	shelled raw prawns
200 g	pork chop meat
200 g	pork liver *or* ox liver
100 g	cooked crab meat
300 g	rice and pea starch noodles *or* rice noodles

Wash bones thoroughly. Grill onion until the outside is slightly burnt. Bring 4 litres of water to the boil in a large saucepan. Add onion, salt and bones. Boil for 20 minutes over fairly high heat, skimming off foam. Reduce heat and simmer for 4–5 hours. Add fish sauce and monosodium glutamate. Test for seasonings.

Prepare prawns as described on p. 12.

Slice meat and liver thinly (about 2–3 mm thick). Place prawns, meat, liver and crab meat in separate piles on a large plate.

Drop noodles into 2 litres of boiling water. When noodles soften, separate them with a fork. Continue boiling for another 5–8 minutes or until noodles are soft. Drain well and rinse under running water.

Keep three burners going at the same time on the stove. On one place a saucepan with boiling water. Pour some of the stock into a smaller saucepan and place it on a burner and bring it to the boil. Keep the soup in the large saucepan simmering.

Place about a handful of noodles in a perforated ladle and dip in hot water to reheat the noodles. Drain well and place them in an individual bowl. Place a handful of bean sprouts, a small lettuce leaf and some crab meat on top.

Place meat and prawns in a ladle and dip it in the small stock saucepan. Stir contents of ladle continuously with a fork or a pair of chopsticks. When meat and prawns are half-cooked, add some slices of liver to the ladle. Stir well until everything is cooked. Pour contents of ladle on top of noodles. Add some more stock if necessary to cover noodles.

Sprinkle with pepper, chopped spring onions and coriander leaves before serving.

Soups & Noodles

SHORT SOUP (WON TON SOUP)
HOANH THANH NAU

	40 won ton wrappings

Filling:

150 g	minced pork
100 g	raw prawns
½ Tsp	salt
1 Tbsp	fish sauce
½ Tsp	pepper
¼ Tsp	monosodium glutamate *(optional)*
	1 onion

Broth:

500 g	pork bones
50 g	dried shrimps
	1 dried squid
	1 onion
2 Tbsps	fish sauce
½ Tsp	salt
1 Tsp	sugar
¼ Tsp	monosodium glutamate *(optional)*
4 L	water

Garnish:

250 g	Xa Xiu *(roast pork)*, sliced *(see p. 32)*
	10 lettuce leaves
	10 spring onions

Prepare broth as described in recipe for Chinese Noodle Soup on p. 82.

To make the filling, first chop onion. Prepare prawns as shown on p. 12. Chill prawns for 30 minutes. Mince prawns in food processor or use mortar and pestle. Mix pork with prawns and seasonings.

Using a table knife, scoop out a small quantity of the pork and prawn mixture (about the size of a cherry), place on a wrapping. Pull all sides of the wrapping together to make a sort of bag. Press the opening tightly. Repeat the process until the mixture is used up.

Prepare spring onions as in recipe for Chinese Noodle Soup on p. 82.

How to Serve:
Boil 4 litres water in a large saucepan. Drop in the won ton balls, about 15 at a time. When the balls float to the surface, scoop them out with a perforated ladle. Drain the water off. Place about 5 balls in each individual soup bowl. Place 2 slices roast pork, half a lettuce leaf, a spring onion stem and chopped spring onions on top. Pour soup on top, enough to cover the contents.

Serve with soya sauce, vinegar, pepper and chilli.

Soups & Noodles

NOODLE SOUP WITH HEART, LIVER AND KIDNEY

HU TIEU NAU LONG HEO

2.5 L	stock
400 g	rice noodles
	1 large onion
200 g	minced pork
½ Tsp	salt
1 Tsp	fish sauce
½ Tsp	pepper
200 g	pig's heart
200 g	kidney
200 g	liver
200 g	bean sprouts
½ cup	chopped spring onions
1 cup	coriander leaves

Prepare stock beforehand, as described in Phnom Penh Noodle Soup, p. 83. Drop noodles in boiling water and continue boiling for about 5 minutes or until noodles are soft. Do not overcook. Rinse noodles with cold running water.

Mince half of the onion and mix it with minced pork, fish sauce, salt and pepper.

Wash heart, kidney and liver and dry well. Slice thinly.

Slice the other half of the onion lengthwise into 5 mm wide sections.

How to serve:
Make sure everyone is seated at the table.

Prepare soup for one person at a time. Heat one teaspoon oil in frying pan over fairly high heat. Add 1 dessertspoon onion. Stir-fry until onion is translucent. Add two or three slices each of kidney and heart. Stir-fry until cooked. Add ½ cup stock and then minced pork. Stir-fry for 1 minute. Add liver, a handful of noodles, a tablespoon of bean sprouts, and stir-fry until liver is cooked. Pour contents into an individual bowl. Add more stock if required. Sprinkle with spring onions and coriander leaves before serving.

RICE AND TAPIOCA FLOUR NOODLE SOUP WITH PORK AND FISH

BANH CANH CA GIO HEO

3 L	water
½ Tsp	salt
	half a leg of pork (about 1.5 kg to 2 kg)
	1 medium-sized mullet
2 Tbsps	oil
	1 onion, sliced
3 Tbsps	fish sauce
¼ Tsp	monosodium glutamate *(optional)*
noodles	*(see recipe p. 81)*
2 Tbsps	chopped spring onions
2 Tbsps	coriander leaves
	pepper

Wash pork leg thoroughly. Remove excess fat and half of skin.

Boil 3 litres water in large saucepan over fairly high heat. Add salt and pork leg, and boil for 20 minutes, skimming off foam. Reduce heat to medium, and boil for 2 hours.

Add fish and boil for 20 minutes.

Remove fish and pork leg from water and drain in a colander. When cool, remove bones from fish. Shred fish into large pieces (about 3 cm wide).

Remove bone from pork leg and slice meat into bite-sized pieces.

Fry onion until fragrant in 2 tablespoons oil over moderate heat. Add fish and 1 tablespoon fish sauce, and stir-fry for 1 minute. Add remaining fish sauce and monosodium glutamate to stock. Test for seasonings. Add pork and stir-fry for 1 minute. Add noodles and boil for 2 minutes.

Serve hot with pepper, spring onion and coriander leaves sprinkled on top.

Soups & Noodles

COMBINATION FRIED NOODLES

MI XAO THAP CAM

300 g	dried noodles *or* 500 g fresh noodles
5 Tbsps	oil
	2 squids
200 g	shelled raw prawns
100 g	crab meat
200 g	lean pork
100 g	pig's liver *or* lamb's liver *(optional)*
	1 set chicken giblets *(optional)*
	1 large onion
1 × 3 cm	piece ginger
	1 carrot
	1 leek
100 g	cauliflower
	2 celery stalks
50 g	bean sprouts *or* cabbage
	2 tomatoes
¼ Tsp	salt
	3 cloves garlic, crushed
2 Tbsps	soya sauce
1 Tbsp	oyster sauce
¼ Tsp	monosodium glutamate *(optional)*
1 Tsp	sesame oil
2 Tbsps	cornflour, mixed with 5 Tbsps water

Boil noodles until soft (dried noodles take about 5–7 minutes. Fresh noodles take 1–2 minutes). Drain and add 1 tablespoon oil to prevent stickiness.

Prepare squids and prawns as described on p. 12. Slice prawns in half. Cut squids as shown on p. 79. Shred crab meat.

Slice meat, liver and giblets thinly.

Cut onion in half lengthwise and then into 8 sections. Cut ginger into matchstick strips. Slice carrot thinly (2–3 mm thickness). Cut leek into 3 cm long pieces. Cut cauliflower into small pieces. Cut celery diagonally into 5 mm thick pieces. Chop celery leaves. Wash bean sprouts. Cut tomatoes in half lengthwise and then into 10 sections.

Heat 1 tablespoon oil over moderately high heat. Add ¼ teaspoon salt. Add half onion and stir-fry until it turns translucent. Add all vegetables except bean sprouts and celery leaves. Stir-fry for 1½ minutes. Add bean sprouts and stir-fry for another minute. Remove and put aside.

Heat another 2 tablespoons oil in the same frying pan. Add the rest of the onion, garlic and ginger and stir-fry until fragrant. Add meat, liver, giblets, prawns and squids. Stir-fry for 5 minutes or until cooked. Add vegetables, soya sauce, oyster sauce and monosodium glutamate.

In another frying pan, heat 1 tablespoon oil over moderate heat. Add noodles and toss for 2 minutes to heat up. Place noodles on a large serving-plate.

Just before serving, add celery leaves, crab meat and sesame oil to the vegetables, seafood and meat mixture, and stir-fry for half a minute. Add cornflour and stir until sauce thickens. Pour mixture on top of hot noodles. If liked, sprinkle with pepper and coriander leaves.

Sauces

Sauces

LEMON SAUCE

MUOI TIEU CHANH

1 Tsp	lemon juice
1 Tsp	vinegar
1 Tsp	salt
¼ Tsp	sugar
½ Tsp	pepper

Mix all ingredients together.

SPICED SHERRY

RUOU NGU VI HUONG

⅓ cup	five spice powder
1 cup	sherry

Mix well in a sterilised jar. Can be stored for later use.

COCONUT AND FISH SAUCE

NUOC MAM THAM

	juice of ½ lemon
1 Tsp	minced fresh lemon grass
3 Tbsps	fish sauce
3 Tbsps	boiled water
1 Tbsp	sugar
1 Tbsp	coconut milk

Mix all ingredients together well.

CARAMEL SAUCE

NUOC MAU

100 g	sugar
	water

Mix sugar with 4 tablespoons water in saucepan. Place saucepan on medium heat to bring it to the boil. Let boil until mixture changes colour. Turn heat down to low, let simmer until brown. Add half a cup of cold water to dissolve caramelised sugar. Stir until sugar is dissolved. Remove from heat and store in a jar for future use.

LEMON AND GARLIC FISH SAUCE

NUOC MAM TOI

	4 cloves garlic, crushed
	juice of 1 lemon
3 Tbsps	sugar
½ cup	fish sauce
½ cup	cold water
	1 chilli, chopped (optional)

Mix all ingredients together.

Sauces

HOISIN SAUCE

SAUCE TUONG DO

1 Tsp	oil
1 Tbsp	hoisin sauce

Stir-fry hoisin sauce in oil for 1 minute.

BLACK BEAN SAUCE—REFINED

SAUCE TUONG DEN

1 Tsp	oil
1 Tbsp	black bean sauce

Stir-fry black bean sauce in oil for 1 minute.

LEMON GRASS AND CHILLI SAUCE

SAUCE XA OT

2 Tbsps	oil
1 Tbsp	finely chopped lemon grass
	3 cloves garlic, crushed
1 Tbsp	chilli powder
¼ Tsp	curry powder
1 Tbsp	roasted sesame seeds, ground
½ Tsp	sesame oil

Heat oil in frying-pan over low heat. Add garlic and fry until golden. Add lemon grass and stir-fry for 1 minute. Turn off heat. Add chilli and curry powder, stir-fry, and add sesame seeds and sesame oil.

Put the three sauces in separate small bowls for dipping beef balls in.

Index